Sarah Howe

Is God enough?

Unexpected invitations to a questioning soul

First Edition, 2021.

Printed in Ireland.

Published by Wild Goose Publishing, Dublin, Ireland.
contact@wildgoosepublishing.ie

Author: Sarah Howe O'Brien
Book title: Is God enough?

ISBN 978-1-5272-7598-0

Design and illustration by Wild Goose Publishing.

For the O'Brien Clan, the Wolf Pack,
any future grandchildren of RE Howe

and

For my *'Tower of Strength and Joy'*...
May the melody in these words sing over you,
gather and weave you together.
Like the beautiful poplar trees outside my window,
May you dance freely with the wind.

"You were within, I was without.
You were with me, but I was not with you.
So you called, you shouted,
you broke through my deafness.
You flared, blazed and banished my blindness.
You lavished your fragrance,
and I gasped."

-St Augustine

Dear Reader,

It's often said that 'hindsight is twenty-twenty'— indeed! Ten years later, I recognize that this book is a record of what others have coined the 'dark night of the soul' or the 'furnace of the beatitudes.'

But then, I had no idea what I was writing...

When we moved Down Under, I had planned to dabble with some writing once my kids were in school. Having two great passions in psychology and theology, I was thinking that it might be fun to write about faith and moving to a new country. Having always been a 'God' kind of person, I figured I had some knowledge I had learned along the way and that perhaps it was time to 'grace' the world with my understanding (Gross, I know!). Suffice to say, I was unprepared for the chess board that was my life to be flipped over. In short, things turned messy! As my journey began to unfold, I found myself in a great spiritual crisis, having to yield once again to what I have called 'the Great Holy Undoing.' Where I thought I knew what I was going to write, where I thought I had arrived and learned answers, instead I had to surrender to the mercy of something far bigger than me.

T.S. Eliot once said: "If the word inspiration is to have any meaning it must mean that the writer is writing something he does not wholly understand."[1]

Indeed, I didn't understand.

For nearly five years, "Write the questions!" is all I could hear; all I could do. Hence, this is not a 'how-to' book. It is not a Christian book of principles to observe in hard times. Nor is it a fairy tale of trouble followed by great triumph, with 'they lived happily ever after' stamped at the end. Rather, it is a gritty book, full of questions, that led me on an unimaginable journey of discovering God afresh.

I read once that sometimes we learn more from asking questions than we ever do from just receiving answers. The following pages then are a 'no frills' kind of record of a five-year spiritual journey. Antipodes, the first section of the book, chronicles the emotional 'earthquake' that followed our move Down Under. The pages that follow that story are a record of me trying to find God in the aftermath; a head to heart journey. As I poured out my heart's doubts, fears and questions, slowly I found myself being 'invited' into a whole new way of seeing and being. I found a map in Jesus' sermon on the plain to

---

1 *tseliot.com*, accessed October 10, 2019, tseliot.com/prose/virgil-and-the-christian-world. pp 122-123

navigate tough territories; poverty, hunger, weeping and oppression. And through it all, I began to discover I was being offered Hope beyond hope.

Warning: There will be lots of Bible verses in bold italicized print. Having been raised in an Evangelical home, I memorised well over 500 Bible verses at an early age. It will be obvious that some of these highlighted verses became a support to my thought process and search for understanding. However, others appear more randomly among my stream of consciousness, popping-up with a voice of their own. Like a boulder that a river must stream around, I have left these verses, flowing my thoughts around them. Furthermore, as I became more and more disoriented by the upside down, I found that these verses would sometimes bring great comfort as they shed light on my situation. While other times, they became something to wrestle with for a deeper, clearer and fuller understanding and need for God. In a way, you could say that these verses became my counsellor, reorienting me to find God anew. While I have highlighted the scripture with bold and italicized print, to keep the flow of writing, I have included all references in the footnotes.

I wrote this for my healing and as a record for my children someday. I hadn't planned to share this with anyone until recently when I received a letter from a young German woman who had just experienced her own deep loss. She wrote and asked if we could meet and talk about 'the pain'. Her following words haunted me:

"...if you have the strength and courage to speak to me about the topic, I would really like to know about your time when you lost a very close person. How you handled it and about what you said to God or if you were angry and how you came back to him. Thank you for that! And Greetings and big hugs Fiona" 9:44am.

Her words made me wonder if there were others who might benefit from my journey. And the fact that she sent her message at 9:44 arrested my attention. This too, you will understand as you read further in these pages.

Jesus said to His disciples: "Whatever I tell you in the dark, speak in the light..."[2]

No doubt your own journey has been very different to mine, but I share mine now in hopes that you, dear reader, will not feel so alone in yours. Certainly, your questions may be different from mine, but it is my hope that by reading this book you will feel empowered to ask your own questions of the living God, as an invitation to dialogue with you. May you find in these pages glimmers of hope, light and courage to keep asking, knocking and seeking Him!

---

2 Matthew 10:2

Contents

up.side.down

1. prologue: a preliminary discourse; a preface or introductory part of a discourse, poem, or novel.
2. upside down: with the upper part under most, in or into complete disorder; topsy-turvy

"I wonder if I shall fall right through the earth? How funny it will seem to come out among the people who walk with their heads downward. –The Antipathies, I think."

-Louis Carroll (Alice in Wonderland)

It was a misunderstanding.

I probably wouldn't have bought a $12 bottle of carbonated water as I did while celebrating our 20th wedding anniversary at a café along Dunedin's Esplanade in St. Clair.

The waitress with the heavy German accent did not ask me, "Would you like mineral water, soda water, or even carbonated water?" Instead, she asked, "Would you like sparkling or just plain old tap water?"

I ask you, "What would you choose?"

"I'll have mine sparkling please!"

I'm not sure what I was thinking. But I was rather surprised when I was handed this plain looking bottle, the 'sparkling' water, with the brand name 'Antipodes' on it. I read the word out loud in my strong American accent; "What do you suppose 'ant-i-podes' means?"

My kiwi husband laughed, "That's pronounced an-tip-o-dees! It is what the English used to call New Zealand, as it is almost the exact opposite spot on the globe from them."

This piqued my interest.

In the native Maori language, New Zealand is known as Aotearoa, meaning *Land of the Long White Cloud*. But how was it that I had been living in this island-nation for over two years and never heard it called by the name Antipodes before?

Since I paid what I considered a steep price for a glass of water, I kept the bottle as a souvenir and stuck it in my kitchen window upon our return home. I had no idea that it would soon be worth every penny I paid thanks to the revelation that it would bring me.

Later that evening, warm sudsy bubbles enveloped my hands as I reached for another dish to wash. I couldn't explain why, but my eyes kept travelling upward, landing on the bottle. It felt as if I was missing something. It wasn't until I dried off my hands and reached for the dictionary that I began to feel a light bulb switch on in my head. I read: *"antipodes: anything that is contrary to, or the exact opposite of something else."*[3]

Sometimes, just one word can bring understanding, giving definition to our present state of being. Physically, geographically, I knew exactly where I was at that moment. I was in Pukerau, a little town outside of Gore, New Zealand, where our family had accepted a 'call' to do ministry at a Christian camp. But my spirit had not been so sure. People use all kinds of analogies to explain the internal landscape of their souls. I have heard them compare their life to being in a valley, a desert or even on top of a mountain; but none of those seemed to fit my own emotional status. Something deep inside was feeling dazed, disoriented and crying out, "Where am I?"

A slight smile of recognition curled up the sides of my mouth. "Ah! I get it! I am in Antipodes!"

I am well accustomed to being a stranger in a strange land; New Zealand is the fourth country I have lived in. But I hadn't anticipated what shifting hemispheres would do.

— Good-bye equilibrium; everything is backwards, or upside down.

---

3 *Webster's New World Dictionary of the American Language*. Everyday Encyclopaedic Edition. Nashville. The Southwestern Company, 1967.

Driving on the opposite side of the road, toilet flushes swirling the other way, light switches turning off and on in opposite directions from the Northern hemisphere…These seemed to be only the beginning of the endless reversals of what I had spent the first 40 years of my life learning.

I wondered, would March, April and May seem like autumn some day? Would I ever want to bring out pumpkins in April? Would I honestly want to make spring bouquets at Thanksgiving? What? NO THANKSGIVING? And winter, winter without Christmas—no lights on the houses or trees to offer hope or warmth for the season?

I didn't realise that I had spent my whole life looking at the world as if through a crystal globe from the top down. In a matter of 24 hours, all perspectives had changed. I now found myself looking at the world from the bottom up. Such change requires a completely different stance and posturing of self on all levels; physical, mental and spiritual.

And there in good old Webster's dictionary was the very word to describe this 'space' I had found myself in. Not only did I literally live in Antipodes, feet planted on the physical inversion of all I had known, but I also found myself living in some strange upside-down state within myself where most of my values had collided with each other.

Life is full of 'about-turns.' Just as we think we know where we are going and picking up speed, a 'switch-direction' sign can be turned on. Maybe you haven't moved to New Zealand. Chances are slim. But maybe you know what it means to find your whole world turned upside down. You know what it means to lose your footing, to have to reposition yourself to meet the demand to be something you have yet to know. Perhaps you have just gotten married, brought home a baby, made a move, or started a new job and found yourself excited for that change, but left dazed, even disoriented by your new surroundings. Some of you have encountered less desirable changes; perhaps you have lost a loved one, battled a serious illness, felt betrayal knife you in the back, laid awake worrying over a wayward teenager, or hoped that you would see God act on your behalf and He didn't, at least not the way you thought He should or maybe needed Him to.

Sometimes when it rains, it pours. Sometimes, when we have barely adjusted to one massive wave of change, another one, a larger one, follows, threatening our very existence. In September 2010, New Zealand shook violently with one of three earthquakes to hit the city of Christchurch. Just six months later in February 2011, three days after we arrived in New Zealand, Christchurch was all but levelled. Sometimes it happens to us, Christ's church, like this.

"Once more I will shake not only the earth but also the heavens." The words "once more" indicate the removing of what can be shaken—that is, created things—so that what cannot be shaken may remain."[4]

In my opinion, one of the hardest things we ever get asked to do as humans is to move one step beyond what we have always known to be true. And yet when we do, we can experience a greater space, a greater freedom than what our previous paradigm permitted.

I had no idea on the day of the second Christchurch earthquake how much my recent international move would shake me. Nor did I know that subsequent 'earthquakes' were imminent. Jesus tried to warn the disciples that He was about to die. But their paradigm of who the Messiah was supposed to be kept them from understanding what he was saying. They would be challenged to move one step beyond what they had always believed to be true.

Are we any different?

I was about to find out that I, for one, was not.

4 Hebrews 12:26b-27

an.tip.o.des

1. a group of islands SE of and belonging to New Zealand.
2. a direct or exact opposite.
3. one whose feet dwell in the land opposite of.

"If I rise on the wings of the dawn, if I settle on the far side of the sea, even there your hand will guide me; your right hand will hold me fast. If I say, "Surely the darkness will hide me and the light become night around me," even the darkness will not be dark to you; the night will shine like the day, for darkness is as light to you."

Psalm 139: 9-11

IT IS WHAT IT IS, AND IT'S A VERY BIG IS

second wave

"Who of us can dwell with the consuming fire?" asked the prophet Isaiah. Is it possible that we should be grateful for God's hiddenness, rather than disappointed?"

-Philip Yancey

Like Lucy stumbling in the wardrobe and happening upon Narnia, the vision came when I was least expecting it.[5]_

We call upon God, but do we expect Him, the Living God, God of Angel Armies, to answer?

He did.

An ordinary morning, alone in this new country, the great South land, I sat down at the kitchen table to have a moment of quiet after the kids went off to school. I closed my eyes, took some time to pause and asked God, "Where are you?" I waited with the eyes of my heart looking, the ears of my heart listening.

I expected him to be as near as He has been in the past.

But this time, He was right across the table.

I opened my eyes.

He was still there, right across from me.

I had the feeling I was at an official meeting, a board meeting. The Lord's eyes were pensive, and I could hear God say what He said to Himself in front of Abraham before me. ***"Shall we hide from her what we are about to do."***[6]

I then noticed that there were four others sitting in my kitchen, one for every place at our six-seat table. The Lord and I sat at the ends. These others looked like soldiers and sat very still, not looking at me or Him,

---

5 *Narnia: The Lion, The Witch and The Wardrobe*, DVD. Directed by Andrew Adamson. Burbank: Disney Pictures and Walden Media, 2005.
6 Genesis 18:17

just straight ahead.

The Lord said they were angels.

An incredible spiritual moment was upon me and I began to tremble and cry.

Fear overwhelmed me.

I don't remember any of the words, but my spirit understood. I saw roots deep in the ground burrowing under a massive rock. I understood that I must cling to Him like never before. I was unsure of the nature of the attack coming, it felt like death, like grievous loss. The soldier-angels visit made the occasion solemn, reminiscent of various movie scenes where soldiers come together to deliver news to a family that their loved one has fallen.

Was the end of the world coming?

How was I to know that it would feel like the end of mine?

My spirit led me to read the book of Isaiah, chapter 32.

In verse 10 it said, *"In just a little over a year from now, you'll be shaken..."*

"...Yes, weep and grieve until the Spirit is poured down on us from above."[7]

More shaking?

Overwhelmed, I fell asleep.

***

Months later, I heard a man named Shane Willard speak words that would offer a soft blanket for my soul to rest in. He told us that Jehovah, the Hebrew name for God when pronounced properly sounded like 'breathing:' *"Yud, He, Vav, He."*[8]

"Yud, He, Vav, He" ... Inhale, exhale, inhale, exhale—we breathe the name of God.

---

7 Isaiah 32:10,15
8 Willard, Shane. 2010. Audio Transcript: Hosting Shane Willard, Shane Willard 2010(3 of 4) http://mikeconnellministries.com/transcript/834/Shane-Willard-2010-3-of-4.aspx?p=10.

He went on to say that the first thing a baby does when it is born is to take a breath, saying the name of God; that it takes the very name of God to sustain life and that when we take our last breath, when we cease to say God's name, we die.

I couldn't have known then how important 'breath' would become. But the words floated gently down deep, tucking themselves away for a later time when they'd be needed.

Then, a miracle happened.

My 'barren' sister gave birth to a little baby girl after ten years of buried hope.

Indigo Rain uttered God's name on her lips with her first breath. She fell from heaven into our arms like dew kissing grass at dawn, reviving our hope in the name of the Living God. Surely our God gives good gifts. Surely our God's arm is not too short to save, to perform miracles.

Good —for we had just discovered that we needed another one!

"Just a quick routine check-up" was all it was supposed to be. That's what they said when my father and sister called. It had been business as usual for them on a late February morning. Starbucks, work and a quick stop at the doctors to confirm that the diagnosis 'cancer free' had not changed. The seven-pound baby size mass that had been making it difficult for my father to catch his breath was found and removed from his chest and had been declared clear at the post three-month check-up. But now, the news was different:

"IT'S BAD," said my sister, "VERY, VERY BAD!"

I burnt the toast, four times, trying to process the stage four terminal cancer death sentence hanging over my father. How do you even begin to think about something that has always been a fixed point, a mountain on which you stand and imagine it suddenly not?

"Though the mountains be shaken, and the hills be removed, yet my unfailing love for you will not be shaken nor my covenant of peace be removed, says the Lord, who has compassion on you."[9]

Dad had just been here, down under, for three weeks over Christmas — such a joyous reunion — so much familiar light and love brought

---

9 Isaiah 54:10

to warm the dark and lonely terrain of my weary soul stumbling along in this new hemisphere.

While visiting, my father, a man of deep insight, listened to me rant about all the changes I had experienced in coming to New Zealand. When I was through, he didn't reprimand me for my ungrateful attitude, instead, he graciously asked, "Hon, can I offer you a suggestion?"

I looked at him, his eyes twinkling as if he knew something that hadn't yet occurred to me. I half rolled my eyes; I did not want to let his kindness diffuse my agitation. I felt justified in my country comparisons and wondered what kind of wisdom he could possibly give me as he had never lived in the Southern Hemisphere. But then again, my father was a highly educated and polished sort of man, who was also extremely down-to-earth and practical; I opened myself to hear what he had to say. He was not one to lecture; short and sweet were his words. – "Love…I don't think it's so much the change from America to New Zealand that you are struggling with as it is from city to rural."

He let me absorb his poignant words. It was true, I had been raised a city girl and did not have any reference point for paved roads suddenly giving way to gravel, long discussions about weather and an extremely pragmatic, no frills kind of culture. The only time I had ever seen a lamb was at a petting zoo, now I was outnumbered by them. When our family drove into the wee town of Pukerau for the very first time, there was a sign on the side of a building that read, *"We buy sheep dags."* When I asked my husband what that meant, he said, "Trust me, you don't want to know the answer to that right now." Having considered myself to be an intelligent and effective communicator, I felt rendered inept at conversation. I had no idea what everyday terms in Southland meant; drenching, dagging, tailing... I might as well have moved to Africa and been trying to learn Swahili, so foreign were the words and ways of the people around me.

Yet as I watched my father engage with the new customs and people of my surroundings; I was in awe. He was brilliant and seemed to be speaking a heart dialect I had never heard; then I remembered that he had been raised a farm boy among the cornfields of Iowa.

"Dad, you have been holding out on me! If I had known what I was coming to, you could have explained a few things to me beforehand." I could tell that Dad was amused.

I joked further, "What's the saying, Dad? You can take the boy out of the country, but not the country out of the boy?" With that, he tipped his sun hat and followed my husband down to the camp's large field.

Next thing I knew, there he was, happily going up and down the fields, riding the camp lawn mower; while a once buried memory within me rose to the surface. Every summer, our family made a long journey from the Canadian plains down to the heartland of America to visit our extended kin. We'd have a week with each parent's family, one in the city, the other in the country. Even now, when I remember our extended family's excitement to see us, hold us, cherish us, I am flooded with the longing of that 'golden' season of life; childhood. It was the warmth of the country farm that flooded back to me that day as I watched my father ride the lawn mower. Suddenly, I could hear the old screen door slam on the back porch as I watched my grandparents come out to greet us; the smell of a ham roast wafting behind them, signalling we'd arrived in time for dinner. After the initial excitement of hugs and kisses and being settled into rooms for our stay, the promise was that if we cleaned our dinner plates, we could go for a tractor ride. Each time, I would scoff my food, and, true to his word, my father would hoist me up onto the big combine at sunset. As if it were yesterday, I recall the sound of a gentle, warm breeze being overtaken by the electrifying roar of the engine, the thrill of my hands on the wheel next to Dad's, thinking that I was driving and the utter safety and security I felt resting in his arms.

Yes, I had almost forgotten that this refined man with 12 years of higher education was a farm boy at heart. Always my captain, he was filled with practical wisdom and knew how to frame things with perspective.

Now, when I heard the news of my stalwart father's cancer, I travelled back to California, praying for a miracle that he might live. I wasn't ready to let go. According to my calculations, Dad should have easily had another 20 years of life in him; that would make him 87, which in my mind was a ripe age for dying, having lived long and well, before becoming decrepit. I was not ready to lose him. I had to let go physically to move across the world from him, but I was not ready to give up my captain. I knew that my dad would have our backs, that he would offer us the sound leadership advice we would need to walk the road ahead of us and that even should we fail, Dad would get us home. Most importantly, I knew that Dad would make a way to see me, his girl.

Besides, there were things, things that I had been watching in Dad's life, wondering about with God, even questioning. I felt that these questions demanded an answer to walk our current road of ministry with confidence. Dad had spent his life in service to God, 48 years of ministry and yet, in his final year of pastoring he had stepped down to a storm of lies, rumours and a manipulative power-hungry evil. In time, I thought, expected, God would clear his name, restore his reputation and position. I was still waiting to see how God would rectify this when the economic downturn of 2011-12 took its toll on Dad's retirement business investments. Two out of the three were lost. He and Mom had retired at the ocean in a little house, it too turned upside down in the market from the fall out and they were forced to leave. Surely, God was not going to end this decade of hardship with death? Hadn't I read in the scriptures that God was the strong deliverer; that He would redeem what the enemy had stolen; that he would use hardship to reveal His glory?

So, I made a resolve; surely cancer is not too big for the likes of God.

Maybe I was in denial.

Inspired by my sister's miracle baby, I resolved to seek God's word on Dad's condition. Each time the doctor would tell us that things were getting worse; I held hope that the doctor's analysis may not be the last word.

Dad, with the family's blessing, decided against chemotherapy that could only promise him a few extra months. If God wanted to heal him then he was open. Otherwise, if it was his time to go, Dad wanted to spend whatever time he had left without being poked, jabbed and sick. He wanted to be with us and to enjoy the remainder of his days, if possible.

The plan was that if or when the pain began to take hold in his body, the nurses would give him morphine. I didn't know that that drug could accelerate our goodbye, and end our time of communication.

And I had no idea how big this forming second wave would become in me. Somewhat dazed, I found myself trying to find places within me to file all the turns of events. Unfortunately, those drawers didn't exist yet. All I could think about the situation was: *'It is what it is... and it's a very BIG IS!'* But this I knew; I was determined to keep my eyes above the waves.

dream

"There is a sacred horror about everything grand. It is easy to admire mediocrity and hills; but whatever is too lofty, a genius as well as a mountain, an assembly as well as a masterpiece, seen too near, is appalling."

-Victor Hugo

In the early California dawn, shortly after Dad started the morphine, I dreamt of him.

My hero's strength was waning. He, who has always held me, was weary from battle and laid his head into my arms. My arms wrapped around his shirtless chest to keep him warm. My eyes surveyed the damage the pirates had done—just "skin and bones," a wisp of the man I had always known. It was clear…the cancerous looters in his chest had begun to pilfer and pillage from his neighbouring organs.

The warrior could not hold up his head. My lips kissed his forehead… and his chest began to heave with deep sobs. "O Daddy, what is it?" I asked. A faint murmur of incoherent words whispered through his dry lips. And I understood. The time for clear communication was nearly over. Transition was upon us.

I awoke with petitions to God for a miracle. It was clear that the decision to start morphine would change things. Should I beg God to spare my father's life when he was so clearly almost dead?

I had pictured the valley of the shadow of death differently. I had imagined it to be like the central valley of California, dry, broad and hot. But my experience of it was more like a deep canyon valley, a stream of water running through with sheer rock face, walls on either side of it. I found myself pushed up close to the base of the canyon; and although I have always admired the Sierra Nevada mountains, even regarded their majesty as seeing the face of God, this was different.

I wrestled to grasp the truth before me: If God is like the mountains and I am pushed up against the base of it, then God has never been so up close and personal, or so unrecognisable.

"He, who dwells in the shelter of the Most High, will rest in the shadow of the Almighty."[10]

I wanted to see God move. Like Moses, I asked God, *"Now show me your glory."*

And the Lord said, "I will cause all my goodness to pass in front of you, and I will proclaim my name, the Lord, in your presence… I will put you in a cleft in the rock and cover you with my hand until I have passed by."[11]

Suddenly timelines blurred, and I remembered myself in a hospital room in transition labour with my littlest one.

What was the nurse asking me? What was she holding up in my face—a chart with faces, something about pain levels? I couldn't hear, respond. I was trying to remember how to breathe.

Fear was pounding on the door with each intensifying wave of pain.

Had they really said I was only at a five? I still had to get to a ten? But it had taken hours to get to a five, all night. Had I really refused pain medication? How would I survive another nine hours of labour? Had we not been praying that God would allow me to experience a natural birth for our fourth child?

Twenty minutes later the nurse's inquisition continued, I could no longer bear to sit in the hard-wooden chair.

I had to change position.

My husband helped me up to my feet. I felt a sudden sensation I had never before or since felt: FIRE! –Not a polite, warming flame, but rather the billows of a rocket engine ignited to launch!

The nurse read my shock. I heard, "Check her progress!"

My friend-turned-midwife walked in and heard the nurse's words, "She's complete!"

The pain was taking me. I was ready to surrender to it when I suddenly saw the whites of my friend's eyes. Firmly, she arrested my attention

10 Psalm 91:1
11 Exodus 33:18-19

from rolling back into the pain and fear that I still had hours of labour to go.

Boldly, she commanded me, "Sarah, take a deep breath for yourself and for your baby… and push!"

I obeyed and felt the relief in the release to push.

Softly came the doula's voice, "Do it again, Sarah!"

And then a holy hush filled the silent night just before the cry of a wee baby girl. And just as the pain seemed unbearable… *it was over*. Little One from heaven was here.

All the fears, all the pain melted in the light of her glory lying at my breast in the holy dawn of Christmas.

We named her Elizabeth Grace Noel, '*Grace promised of God on Christmas*'.

Once again, my dream seemed to indicate another form of transition was upon us.

In our current transition of life to death, was there a promised grace to be held? What miracle should be requested? Instead of asking for God to spare my father, perhaps I should ask that his death might defy normal procedures as in the birth of my Little One? Perhaps, I should ask that things might accelerate at a rate that would be manageable for him to endure?

I understood that my heart was about to experience the ring of fire.

I prayed for a miracle.

I prayed that he would live, or that he would die quickly.

But most of all I prayed that I would see, with my eyes and heart, God passing by. That during this time, I would have eyes to see all of God's goodness and life needed to empower me to live out the rest of the days ordained for me. Truly, I had no idea the journey that this prayer would take me on.

And I hoped.

And I wondered… What will I name that which is being born in my father's dying?

hope

"Faith is being certain of what we hope for; certain of what we do not see."

-Hebrews 11:1

In the wee hours of the morning at my mom's house in California, our temporary bedroom door banged open, jarring me from my sweet slumber. My sister's voice crashed in on my dreams, breathless, helpless and urgent. I found myself running blindly down the stairs before my brain had fully processed her words, *"It's happening!"*

My body knew this drill, it had already happened once. My brain was trying to figure out what was happening this time. Was it the same as last time? *"Come quick, Dad has fallen."*

The last time, this race had ended at the bathroom door, jammed by a body that lay wedged between it, the toilet and two walls. *Father*! The strong and dignified Preacher Man lay bare and helpless on the ground. And I breathed: adrenaline pumping, heart pounding, 'knees-threatening-to-give-way' prayers.

"God never closes a door, without opening a window." Wasn't that what the Reverend Mother in the Sound of Music told Maria?

The window! I ran outside. Yes, there was the world's tiniest window. Could it be unlocked?

Hope surged,

Grace granted,

An opening made.

My husband, obviously the strongest, opted to go in first, but could not squeeze through. My little sister, a professional velvet heart in caring for the elderly, knew exactly what to do as she manoeuvred her tiny frame through the window. Under and up, she pulled Preacher Man into her.

For a moment, I was frozen by the scene.

Like a baby leaning against his mama's breast, my father let my sister cradle him. *And suddenly, the tables had turned in the parent-child relationship.* Long after he was securely tucked back into his bed, the aftershocks kept coming. I knew deep down that *nothing would ever be the same again.*

Like my dream seemed to indicate, morphine slowly reduced the man to a child—a toddler struggling to communicate his needs. And I wrestled within my soul…

"Is there nothing to be done God?"

"Are you not the same God yesterday, today and forever?"

Are you not the OMNIPOTENT, OMNISCIENT, OMNIPRESENT God? *Don't such big words need to be backed by action?*

And I remembered the words of James: ***Faith without works is dead![12]***

And so, I determined that I would not let my father die without petitioning heaven for a miracle, a creative solution, a window to open.

I spoke to a wise man. I asked him, with doubt reeking from my pores, "Have you ever known anyone to survive advanced stages of cancer?

-Really?

-Truly?

-Fully?

'Yes."

He answered "YES!" This wise man had prayed for and known a woman to recover fully from this ravenous beast of a disease. But then he grew quiet, pensive, as if searching for something amongst the archives of his experience, before he spoke again:

"You know, sometimes God can still do a miracle, but not necessarily with the outcome you hope. I was called to pray for a man whose stomach was so riddled with cancer that it had blown up like a balloon. As I prayed, I watched the man's abdomen shrink and the pain leave him…"

12 James 2:17

I felt hope rise before the wise man added, "He died three days later."

He then challenged me: "Do you trust the ways of God?"

Who has known the mind of the Lord or been his counsellor?"[13]

Who can know the full outcome of what God has planned?

I hoped. I wanted my father to hold me again with strong arms.

I hoped. I wanted to see God perform a miracle. If he could heal my father from cancer, it would be the same, in my mind, as seeing the dead rise. *Just imagine* what my father, once a Preacher Man could be, should he know God not only in His suffering, but also in His resurrection power! Just think of all the faith that could be stirred should he live.

And I recalled Abraham with the Lord, deliberating over the outcome for Sodom.

IT'S NOT OVER UNTIL IT'S OVER! I hoped and prayed for life. Anything had to be better than what we were dealing with.

As I prayed, I saw in my mind's eye a stranger, a man, coming to pray for my father.

"Seriously God??? How might that happen?"

Two days later, a good friend came to visit my father and me. As she left, I asked her the same question I had asked the wise man, "Have you ever known anyone with advanced stages of cancer to be actually, really, truly, fully healed?"

"Yes!"

Again a 'YES'! She said, "Yes, I know a man named Roger. He once lay twisted and gnarled up in his bed, paralysed by the shattered vertebrae from the stage four tumours that began in his liver and pancreas. He is now walking."

AGAIN, HOPE SURGED!

---

13 Romans 11:34

Two nights later, some old friends of ours invited us to dinner. We met their other dinner guests, strangers, a man and his wife. As it turned out, this man happened to be the "Roger" that my other friend had just spoken about. And this stranger now turned acquaintance heard about my father and said, "Let me come pray for your dad tonight!"

Again, GRACE granted…

Again, an Opening was made…

And then…

NOTHING!

For seven days nothing happened. Dad lay there listless, confused and unable to be understood by us. On day seven, Dad, for some unknown reason, refused to take his morphine. He quit cold turkey. We were told later that this alone could have killed him. My brother, a recovered meth addict himself, sat with and tended to Dad, the Preacher Man; like Moses before the burning bush, I knew I was on Holy Ground.

Slowly Dad regained himself and his mind; He actually seemed to be healing. I had tickets to return to New Zealand in a week. Should I go or extend them?

A kindred spirit in Chicago who knew of the situation and was praying wrote to me, "Extend your ticket!"

Still I was not sure. *"God, define things for us, please!"*

And then the present event began, the BANG of our temporary bedroom door.

"It's happening!" And the running began.

We arrived at Dad's bedside. And the horror temporarily paralysed us with fear. Preacher Man was bug-eyed and desperately gasping for air, a man drowning in the unseen. For nearly three hours, Death seemed to thrash him till he was blue in the face. The Medicine Man came and gave him a shot. My husband prayed Jesus' words to Lazarus, "Ronn, come forth!" And then, rather suddenly, Death's choke hold released.

Dad pulled forward, took a big gulp of air and began to stabilize. Baby pink crept back into his cheeks, his eyes began to focus and his words returned, leaving us all stunned.

"What happened?" he asked.

He didn't know. I heard the Medicine Man mutter under his breath the word, 'hypoxia,' as if a question to himself. I didn't know what that meant, but I took comfort in knowing that Dad hadn't really felt the horror of what we had witnessed; it is amazing how the body knows how to protect the true self.

Again: Hope surged, grace was granted and an opening seemed to be made.

thinning veil

"What an awakening one who has walked with Him in the twilight must have, when suddenly she awakes in His likeness and the light is shining around her—all shadowing ways forgotten."

-Amy Carmichael

We had watched Preacher Man gather strength. Dad's hair grew back in black, his appetite returned; he was able to hold the baby and laugh with his grandkids. And after witnessing Dad's revival from the very clutches of Death itself, it felt like we were seeing nothing short of a miracle. Clearly, if God wanted to heal him, he could.

Now I was *really* confused: should I stay or go? I had a life on hold in New Zealand. If God was healing him, I could return. If not, I would need to extend my ticket. I wrote my praying friend in Chicago again of all that had transpired since she had encouraged me to extend my ticket. She wrote again:*"Extend your ticket. All the words you have been given have been fulfilled. Prepare, as it is time for your father to go home. When it's time, it will be peaceful. I see him lying comfortably with a white sheet covering him."*

I tucked her words away in my heart.

"And Mary... pondered all these things..."[14]

I asked God, "If what she says is true, could I, like Elisha who asked to see Elijah depart, see my father go? I want to be there when he makes his last exhale. And I want to know beyond a shadow of a doubt that it's you God that has him."

And I knew that this request held more than just a goodbye for me. As a child I had been extremely ill. Years afterwards, I had had a dream and an encounter that I had held in a deep place in me:

There was a knock at my front door. When I opened it, there stood two elderly ladies with grey hair swept back into tidy knots at the back of

---

14 Luke 2:19

their head. I thought that they were church ladies; along with them was a little brunette girl with big blue eyes. I greeted them with a 'hello' but immediately felt danger, something about them wasn't right. Their eyes were green, shaped like cats, they stared without blinking, as if that was all the return greeting needed. Fear gripped me and immediately I moved to slam the door shut. Only the little girl shoved her arm in the way before I could fully close it. Then I awoke, with my heart pounding, my body temporarily paralysed.

I whispered to God, "Where are you?"

"I am right here!"

"Who were those ladies God?"

"Sickness and Death."

"And the girl?"

"The little girl was you."

"What shall I do God?"

"Look at your dream again with me. Don't be afraid."

I looked at the door from my dream. It was closed but bulging with the threats from these benign looking, but clearly demonic creatures.

I heard God say, *"Don't be afraid. Open the door again and stand back. What happens?"*

I was perplexed. "I don't understand God, nothing is happening. They are just standing there!"

"Right Sarah! Although they may sometimes be allowed to touch you. They can't claim you; you are mine. They can only intimidate and threaten you. Now take back the girl."

I grabbed the girl from the clutches of Sickness and Death without much of a struggle. She wanted to come with me.

I looked back to the Lord. He said, *"Remember Sarah, Sickness and Death are not from me."*

"I don't understand God. I am sure I will get sick again and someday I will have to die. Everybody does eventually."

"You live in a fallen world. Sometimes you will feel the effects of the world's state. But understand this: When it comes time for you to die, it is I that will come for you!"

If this were true, then wouldn't God do the same for Dad? I had to know. If possible, I wanted to see with my own eyes. Clearly, sickness had been allowed to touch him. And the night before, it had seemed as if death had tried to have a go.

What would happen?

That evening, my sister grabbed her guitar and we gathered around Preacher Man to sing and pray him to sleep. Again, the middle of the night brought on another episode nearly the same as the first. This time our medicine man friend said that he thought that Dad's tumours had most likely spread to his brain, interfering with his autonomic nervous system and starving his brain of oxygen.

And I wondered if the veil between heaven and earth was not thinning as I was left wrestling with two things that I saw with the eyes of my heart. First, my father's mother who had died from tuberculosis when he was only 3 years of age was there and seemed to be imploring the Lord. She grabbed hold of his arm and seemed to be reminding him of an agreement they had. I rubbed my eyes. Surely, I had a vivid imagination!

Then, I saw the soldier-angels from the vision just a little over a year before in my kitchen. They walked in, in single file. The first angel turned towards me and tipped his hat, then the soldiers took their place at Dad's bedside.

I didn't know what to think.

On the third and final night, Dad began a third episode. This time was different. He sat up, his eyes bulging and began to point while trying to speak. He managed to utter, "Ma!" We yelled for my mother to come. As she walked in, Dad became agitated and tried to wave her aside. Again, he pointed beyond my mother and managed the word "Ma!" before he laid back into his elevated hospital bed. Suddenly, he seemed quite peaceful on that hot July evening; we pulled up just his sheet to tuck him.

Everyone dispersed for bed.

I turned and looked at Dad. He was lying peacefully with a white sheet over him, just as my friend had said and I knew to stay and watch for a while.

An hour later, I went to get my sister. She woke with a fright and I quickly reassured her that Dad was still sleeping peacefully.

"What then?" she asked.

"I don't know. Just come watch with me."

We snuggled into each other by Dad's bed. A few minutes later, my sister noted that Dad was sitting in what she called the happy baby pose: "That's how Indie (her miracle baby) sleeps on me when she is content and safe. Do you think that maybe his mom is holding him?" she asked.

Hadn't Dad pointed to "Ma!"??? Hadn't I seen his mother speaking to the Lord the morning before? Was that what the agreement had been between the Lord and my father's mother? Had she asked to be able to be with him in his last hours, hold him, knowing what it was like to not be able to breathe from her own death?

Do things like this happen? This was way beyond any theology I had been handed.

At 4am, my sister, who works with the elderly and deals with death and dying on a regular basis said that if Dad was going to die, it would take hours. His breathing was not laboured enough. I felt in my spirit that it wouldn't be long. Perhaps like the birth of my daughter, his death would defy normality for the sake of his endurance?

I couldn't take my eyes off him.

Twice, he made facial expressions that we had seen him make with the grandchildren. It was an expression that showed his great pleasure. And I wondered if he was seeing something we couldn't? Just a few weeks before, I had asked him, "Dad, do you think it's time for you to go home? Are you seeing the veil thin between heaven and earth?"

35

Not a man ordinarily given to emotionalism, I was surprised to see his eyes fill with tears. He struggled to hold his voice steady, before he answered tenderly: "Last night I saw Rachel's children and Jacob."

At first, I thought he was talking about Bible characters. Then I realised that he meant my miscarried son, Jacob, and the unknown, unnamed miscarried children of my sister, Rachel. He continued, "They were waving at me — "Hi Grandpa!" They are waiting for me."

I didn't know what to think then, other than perhaps I shall like heaven after all. I tucked the memory inside. But if Dad's mother was now with him, holding him, could Jacob and the other children be present as well?

Dad coughed violently and sputtered twice.

It woke my mom sleeping in my parent's bed next to Dad's hospital bed. I told her that I thought it might be nearing time. She joined us in watching. She mused, "Wouldn't it be something if he died on the 44?" It had become amusing to the family that every time someone had asked me what time it was, it happened to be on the forty-fourth mark.

"That's almost a bit creepy, Sarah," Mom would say.

We would all laugh, "I know, right? –I think God's just letting us know that He is with us in all these crazy moments."

8:44, 10:44, 12:44…God can be very personal. He knows how to speak in little ways to make His mark in each of our lives.

The number 44 had become one of those personal things between God and me.

While I still lived in America, I told God that I wanted my days, my time, to be about him. I had made several life choices and adjustments at that time and asked God for assurance that he was with me. Then a strange thing began to happen, every time I would go to check the time, it would seem to be on the twenty-second minute of the clock. At first, I thought it was a coincidence, but then I noticed a pattern. In moments that I needed to be reassured, inevitably when I would glance at the clock it would be at the 22. So, I began to see the number 22 on the clock like a wink from God. It became a way that I felt certain that

God was with me and that I was either doing or being right where I needed to be in that moment.

Just before I found out that we were going to move to New Zealand, I was awoken at 2:22 early one morning. I smiled at the time and then heard God say, "I am going to take you from the 222 to the 444." I had no idea what it meant but managed to mumble an "Okay!?" before falling back asleep. A short time later, I found out that we were moving and sure enough, I began to see the 44 for the same kind of assurance that the 22 used to bring.

At 4:21am, without any obvious fanfare, Dad's chest stopped moving.

"Rachel, Mom... look!"

Surprised that there had not been any prolonged laboured breathing that is customary in these types of situations, my sister jumped to her feet, aware that my brother would want to be with us.

I felt a strange form of dismay. Was this it—no 'personal' sign for the mess we found ourselves in? I had hoped that if I stayed and watched, like Elisha, that I would see God in some greater way. My father was a Christian; he had received Jesus into his life at a young age. I, too, had put my trust in Jesus. In our belief system, we held great hope for what was next and were excited for Dad to meet his Jesus face to face; there was no doubt about heaven or that my father would go there. But I wanted something beyond mere belief, I had been contending for more. I wanted *to see* God in it all in a very personal way! Maybe it was wrong, but I wanted a sign that what God had told me in my dream years ago, was true—that He would indeed be the one to come and get us when it was time.

At 4:22am, my sister turned to get my brother. Just as she began to leave the room, we heard it. She turned around. All three of us looked at Dad. His face was peaceful as he exhaled his last breath, one final declaration of the name of God from his lips on this earth—*Yud He Vav He,* ...and then he was gone.

Dad's official time of death was 4:22am.

My heart jumped. Of course, it was 22! We were, after all, in America.

A wave of profound assurance washed over me as I heard a whisper deep in my spirit: *"It's me. I got your dad.* ***"Forget the former things; do not dwell on the past. See, I am doing a new thing! Now it springs up; do you not perceive it?"[15]***

I didn't know then that the verse that followed this instruction was a promise for where I would have to walk, ***"I am making a way in the desert and streams in the wasteland."[16]***

An unusual sound pitter-pattered on the roof just as Dad passed. We flung open the outside door to discover rain falling, disrupting months and months of drought. Sun silvered the edges of the clouds, a few beams bursting forth with some indescribable glory.

Every day leading up to Dad's death, we had read the Psalm for the day. We came back in and read the 19th Psalm: ***"The heavens declare the glory of God..."[17]***

To look outside, it was if God was illustrating his word. Had I not asked for God to show me His glory?

What was I asking?

What kind of glory?

---

15 Isaiah 43:18
16 Isaiah 43:19
17 Psalm19:1

eulogy

"O Captain! my Captain! our fearful trip is done,
The ship has weather'd every rack, the prize we sought is won,
The port is near, the bells I hear, the people all exulting,
While follow eyes the steady keel, the vessel grim and daring;
But O heart! heart! heart!
O the bleeding drops of red,
Where on the deck my Captain lies,
Fallen cold and dead."
-Walt Whitman

The days after were a blur.

Thankfully, Dad was a planner and knew this girl well.

A few weeks before his death, he pulled me aside.

"Love, you're the eldest, I want you to do the eulogy at my funeral."

He saw my hesitation, then gently took hold of my hand before saying, "I know that you are still hoping for a miracle, but I think that it would be wise to be prepared. It's hard to think in grief, so I want you to write my obituary and eulogy for me this week."

Always, Dad was thinking ahead for what his family might need; I felt my stomach turn at the thought of Dad not living. I tried to imagine his funeral and standing before the crowd in such a vulnerable state of grief and then a dread of great proportions gripped my heart. My father had been a man of community; and quite suddenly, I was aware that there would be people there who didn't support Dad or even love him, perhaps even those I would consider enemies.

I stammered, "Dad, w-w-what, what if the people who have made your life so difficult are there?"

Total peace washed over Dad's face, "You don't need to worry about them love, God's got them too. Let's let Him be the judge of it all. I don't need to defend myself and neither do you."

And so, I went away to write for the day.

How do you sum up a man's life—especially when he is one of the most important people in the world to you? How do I define my father's life, when I can't define my very self without him?

I began by trying to be objective, there would be a lot of people at the funeral. But I had a hard time keeping it there:

A.W. Tozer, author of <u>The Pursuit of God</u>*, once said:*

"The man who has God as his treasure has all things as in one… and he has it purely, legitimately and forever."[18]

I can think of no greater quote to sum up the life of my father. As I attempt to summarize his 67 years into a few sentences…the driving theme, that thread of truth through every stage in his life and even in his death, was that Dad treasured God.

Ronald Evans Howe was born Feb. 17, 1945 in Northern Iowa. His early years were not without trauma. His mother died from tuberculosis when he was just three years, leaving three little boys under the age of four to their farmer father. God's protection and grace literally brought along a young woman named Grace, who loved these boys as her own. The young Christian family grew from three to nine children, making Dad the second to the eldest (and now the first to go of all his siblings). His early tales were of a one room schoolhouse, Sunday dinners and playing pioneers with his brothers in the woods on their acreage.

Dad loved to learn and knew how to work hard. At the age of just nineteen years, after one year of study at Moody Bible Institute in Chicago, Dad took his first church on the edge of the Sand Hills in North Nebraska for a 3-month summer pastorate. And from there, over the next forty-eight years, God allowed him to preach around the world. However, education remained important to him. Dad did go back to school after that summer pastorate and did another eleven years in college and graduate school training for the ministry God had for him.

Although his first love was preaching the word, he always felt ministry could or would occur wherever he might be, as the living God lived inside of him. Therefore, whether he was driving buses in Chicago,

18 Aiden Tozer. *The Pursuit of God.* (Kent; STL Books, 1976)

practicing law in Dallas, working as a chaplain for a CFL team in Canada, pastoring churches, or most recently being the CEO of a growing healthcare company in Fresno, his heart was to bring glory to God. Being a forward thinker and having a heart for missions, Dad particularly enjoyed being among the nationals of some of the third world countries he was able to visit and preach in and was working on ways to have his business run in such a way as to fund further mission excursions to these places.

Dad was a man of action. He made decisions and did not look back…he kept his eyes forward and on Jesus. In 1970, Dad met and married the love of his life after dating just four months. Being the man of action, three children promptly followed within the next few years…along with a move to the far North of Canada's midwest territories where he would pastor a church for 10 years. In 1985, our family would move to Fresno, California where Dad would pastor the Fresno Evangelical Free Church for the next 18 years and begin the first long term care facility in the valley for those with Alzheimer's and dementia. In the most recent years, Mom and Dad enjoyed living in Shell Beach, being a part of the California West Coast Wedding Association and Dad took great joy from relating with the men in his covenant group.

And as I read you these accomplishments and details of Dad's life, they seem hollow—mere details.

As his little girl, I want to blurt out that he loved the colour blue, the smell of books and his Starbucks Grande decaf to the top. Fresh strawberry rhubarb pie was his favourite; he smelt of Irish spring and quorum. He was a rare gentleman, gracious and in my mind of a breed of men that seem to be a dying species. He was allergic to pineapple and hated the red tape of bureaucracy and long lines. His hands were always soft and supple…as was his heart. He loved his wife, his children and was committed to making memories with us. He took his role as protector seriously. My sister, Rachel, recalls Dad flying out to Nashville to escort her on her cross-country road trip home, making sure to stop at all the national parks along the way. Dad was also a great supporter and encourager to each of us. My brother, Mike, remembers Dad believing in him as an artist even though his career choice was not traditional or conventional and credits Dad for the artist he is today.

I have been so fortunate to have such a wonderful father, but perhaps the greatest thing I have taken from him is how he revered God, how he treasured his God. Often with curiosity, I would watch him struggle with how to live with eternity in his heart, here and now. I witnessed him go from wanting to be a man of God, to God making him the real deal. I saw him try to emulate his model Jesus and great temptations thrown in his path to deter his course. My favourite story of Dad as a young man was of him showing up to a meeting at a law firm. The head honchos wanted to hire him, but also saw that he was a seminary student. The boss said, "We'd love to welcome you to this firm, but just one quick detail needs to be clarified; we see that you are a seminary student, in this firm we worship the almighty dollar first and will expect the same of you." Dad refused the job.

Like Jesus, his master, he knew moments of great favour, but was also not spared from betrayal and the crowd turning against him. To this I would hear him say and wrestle with the religious demon, "The Lord is my light and salvation; whom shall I fear? The Lord is the strength of my life; of whom shall I be afraid?[19]

And I saw the Lord give and take away. Perhaps the most memorable moment of faith I have ever seen witnessed was one bleak thanksgiving. Dad read aloud, "though the fig tree does not bud and there are no grapes on the vines, though the olive crop fails and the fields produce no food, though there are no sheep in the pens and no cattle in the stalls, yet I will rejoice in the Lord, I will be joyful in God my Saviour. The Sovereign Lord is my strength; he makes my feet like the feet of a deer; he enables me to go on the heights."[20] And I knew where he stood: He would trust and believe that his treasure was enough, that it would sustain us. And God was faithful…and I began to trust that God was the worthiest investment ever.

Finally, I would like to close by sharing one of my most treasured memories with Dad. I had just miscarried our second child during my second trimester of pregnancy. My husband was out of town for the weekend, so I went to stay with my parents after being released from the hospital. Early on a Sunday morning, I discovered that Dad had cancelled his preaching, something I had not recalled him ever doing

19 Psalm 27:1
20 Habakkuk 3:17-19

before; when I stumbled out of bed and wandered into the living room where I could hear old gospel music playing. Dad was sitting on the couch in his robe. I took one look at him and suddenly he seemed small, vulnerable and I knew that I was catching a glimpse of the little boy that been left without his mama. There I was, a devastated mama without her baby boy. I looked at Dad and said, "Do you think your mama is holding my boy?" And then, the sweetest of moments, we cried and held each other. For a moment my empty mama's arms were filled with my father, the little boy without a mama.

Now, for Dad things have come full circle. He has moved into the forever part. He is with his mama, my son and many others...waiting for me and the rest of us too. And I can't help but think that his feet are strong and walking on the high places.

"The man who has God as his treasure has all things as in one and he has it purely, legitimately and forever!"

And even now, I wonder if that eulogy did him justice. There was so much more I could have said to convey his nature, yet words fail me and tears betray me.

How can I capture the sound of his voice, the touch of his hand, his insightful manner, his steadfast nature? And as if an answer, memory washes over me. I couldn't have been more than five or six years old. Every so often I would awake in the night and a feeling of dread would begin to rise in me. I didn't know that I was hallucinating from the anti-seizure medication I was taking; I just knew that the dots would start. Dots would begin to travel diagonally from the left ceiling corner of my bedroom to the adjacent right-hand floor corner. They would come in waves of colour, first red, then yellow, then green, blue...and all the while I could feel my anxiety creep higher. I knew what started beautiful would give way to something sinister; yellow eyed snakes drilling holes in my walls, hissing through fangs, their way towards me. But I could not escape, because just then miniature people would begin to appear, walking alongside my arm in bed; I could crush them should I roll over and even if I could make it past them somehow, I knew there was a monster under my bed that would suck me under. If by some miracle, I could make it out of bed and to the hallway, there were little men working on the ceiling, knocking chunks of debris to the ground. And most terrifying was the vision I had through the hallway linen closet to the outside world. Everything was on fire, as if the apocalypse had taken place and I was left feeling helpless as I watched my best friend's house in flames across the street.

Terror would grip me in such a way that I would become paralysed. Fear would not let me use my voice; I would try to scream out but all I could manage was a very faint, raspy — "Daa-ad."

I don't know how, but one night, Dad heard in his spirt and came. To my little heart, he braved the falling sky, the fire, the snakes, the monster and the little people to get to me; in an instant, all the horror disappeared. Suddenly, light zapped the snakes and other creatures and I, this little saucer-eyed girl, felt the warmth and safety of Dad wrapping his arms around me. Gently, his words reassured me and I felt the blood begin to flow to my extremities again. He carried me back to their room that night and I slept safe and sound cocooned between my mother and father.

I'm a big girl now. And yet, I feel the tearing of that sweet cocoon that I have always known I could run back to if I needed. And with that I can feel some sort of deep disappointment seep into my soul. Dad was only 67 years old. We should have had another 20 years. *Why didn't you heal him, God?*

"Hope deferred makes the heart sick."[21]

Hope is defined as the feeling that what is wanted can be had or that events will turn out for the best. –I certainly did not get what I had hoped for and it doesn't feel like things have turned out for the best.

A storm has threatened my soul and I wonder how I shall emerge from it. I have heard that the way forward is sometimes the way back? What could that possibly mean? At the very least, I suspect I may not understand any of this until the clouds clear?

"Then the Lord said, "There is a place near me where you may stand on a rock. When my glory passes by, I will put you in a cleft in the rock and cover you with my hand until I have passed by. Then I will remove my hand and you will see my back…"[22]

---

21 Proverbs 13:12
22 Exodus 33:21-23

Perhaps the glory of God can only be seen in hindsight, when what has been blocking our vision is removed and we can see where He has passed by us?

Are you passing by me now, God?

I can't feel, hear or see any response. Only a verse comes to mind:

"My soul waits in silence for God only...For my Hope is from Him."[23]

Maybe it is only when our hope has been deferred, when we find ourselves standing in Antipodes, shaken to the core, that we are challenged to look to *the Hope beyond hope*?

Is this what I am to name what is being birthed through my father's death: *Hope beyond hope*?

I resolve to stand steadfast, to be strong in this season.

As predicted, there was a large public funeral, nearly 2,000 came. A week later, we had a private family burial of Dad's ashes at sea and then, as odd as it seemed, went to lunch.

So, life went on even without the captain, the man with perspective.

Perspective?

"The Lord gives and He takes away...blessed be his name."[24]

The phrase first uttered from the mouth of Job is easy to say, but another thing to yield one's life to.

It was one year, four months and two days later, *just a little over a year* from when the Captain of the Heavenly Hosts and His strong men came to my kitchen, that we watched our Father take his last breath. And little did I know what was set to follow.

---

23 Psalm 62:5
24 Job 1:21b

45

pov.er.ty

1. the state or condition of having little or no money, goods, or means of support; condition of being poor.

2. deficiency of necessary or desirable ingredients, qualities

3. scantiness; insufficiency

"You're blessed when you've lost it all. God's kingdom is there for the finding."

Luke 6:20

AFTERMATH YEAR ONE:
WHERE'S GOD IN MY DARKNESS; WILL HE LET GO IF I DO?

surrender
an invitation to 'be still'

"The strong are not always vigorous, the wise not always ready, the brave not always courageous, and the joyous not always happy."

-C.H Spurgeon

After returning to Down Under, I wanted to be courageous like the wintering naked trees outside my periwinkle living room walls.

There they stood, tall, straight…regal.

No apologies were made for their vulnerable state as they yielded to the time and to the season. And from what I understood, all the while, their roots plunged into greater depths beneath the frosted surface.

They didn't seem to be worried about losing their leaves or when they might come back. They didn't seem to be trying to speed up the season. They didn't seem to be doing any kind of labour, except for yielding.

I wanted to yield to heaven and trust in the unfailing love and goodness of the Ancient of Days.

I wanted to stand with that kind of elegance and dignity in this bare season.

I wanted to be gracious in death and noble in accepting my world being turned upside down.

And I tried.

But, in reality, if I'm honest, it has felt more like we have all begun to spiral downward. And my hope has been that like Alice's entrance into Wonderland, we might be falling upward?

***

Three months after Dad's death, it's been a difficult day.

Already it has been hours…

She's not giving up, she's giving in. Her head rolls back. Prim, our pet lamb, has been on her side fighting for her life, her breath labouring. Suddenly her four legs kick wildly into the air, her eyes moving frantically to and fro, before she freezes.

My Little One begins to cry, her heart sensitive to the lamb's suffering. Little Man has his back to me, standing staunch, arms crossed. I send Little One to get her daddy.

Little Man turns to see if I am still there. My concerned gaze is met with swollen red-rimmed eyes defying me to ask any questions. He does not want to be asked, "How are you feeling?" I hesitate and then stand directly behind him and place my hand on his shoulder. He collapses into me with deep sobs.

Sometimes there are no words.

My memory recalls a Sunday morning service. Voices were waking as they dutifully sang the choruses when the instruments took over.

And the notes from the piano began to…

Crescendo, Fall and Swirl around me

Goose pimply flesh, hair vertical on the nape of my neck

The Holy Spirit come

Rippling through every cell of my being

No defined thoughts

No words

Just His presence,

to revive my weary, grief-stricken soul.

Sometimes there are no words. – Only a presence.

"Be still and know that I am God."[25]

---

25 Psalm 46:10

Woman Child and Man Child have been weeping all day as the death of our pet lamb, Prim, becomes imminent, bursts of anger pouring up out of their wounded hearts. "Why does God keep letting things like this happen?"

Their teen venom and bits of profanity act as a poor bandage to the gaping wound left by so much loss; friends, family, home, community, church and their basic understanding of how life works.

Moving was hard, but death is final.

Prim dies on the third month anniversary of our beloved Grandpa's death.

Daddy arrives. The lamb's ear perks up to the resonance in his voice. She gives one last valiant kick, fighting to stay with us, before stillness sets in. Daddy checks her heart, it is still beating. We wait in the quiet, Daddy's hand on her heart. It is agonizing to watch her suffer and we breathe a sigh of relief when his hand is removed. It's over.

And suddenly it is no longer Oct 19th, but July 19th, 2012, 4:22am.

And I remember the sudden silence,

the holy hush over the room,

God's hand upon my father's heart calling him home,

One last exhale,

Heartbeat arrested,

Throat rattle quieted,

Hum of the oxygen tank stilled,

The struggle for life, now over.

My father, their Grandpa, was still and now knows God in full. But the rest of us are writhing in pain, grasping to make sense of it all.

If hope is not in an outcome, but a BEING, what do we do when we are not sure we can trust that BEING? I hear their question echo in the deep recesses of my own soul, "Why does God keep letting things like this happen?"

Certainly, *the world is not 'as it should be'*. Death, darkness and decrease are allowed to advance and scale fortified walls. They cross over into those who would live for light, life and increase, ravaging the faithful.

I am learned. I have been taught.

I have theories. I have theology.

But their question resounds in my bones and I yield, I surrender. I choose to be still and wait for the *Presence that Swirls* to substantiate theories.

This is a season for: –

      -lessons to be made into understanding…*again*

        -theories to become personal encounter…*again*

         -and theology to become faith...*again*

I once read that we learn more from asking questions than we do from having the answers. Today is not a day for answers, but a time to let the questions seep into the deep. Not a day for talking but listening.

Is it true that there "*are two kinds of doubt: one that fully lives into the questions and one that asks the questions as weapons against fully living?*"[26]

If so, God, can you direct the questions?

Is it true that we can find light in your eyes even in our dark?

Is it true that your breath can sustain us?

Will you force oxygen into our veins, keep us alive, even if we struggle to say your name?

> **The Lord is good to those whose hope is in him,**
> **to the one who seeks him;**
> **it is good to wait quietly**
> **for the salvation of the Lord.**[27]

---

26 Ann Voskamp (2013). "The Greatest Gift: Unwrapping the Full Love Story of Christmas", p.156, Tyndale House Publishers, Inc.
27 Lamentations 3:25-26

energy
an invitation to learn the unforced rhythms of grace

"What is to bring light must endure burning."

-Victor Frankl

It is a simple, but peculiar question.

The counsellor lifts her hands up for me to see and asks, "Are you fire?"

I had come to her looking for some sort of answers to all the convoluted thoughts that had coiled themselves up into some tight ball in my mind. I thought perhaps if I could hear myself talk out loud, I could begin to separate this complicated knot of grief that had developed in the overseas move and been compounded by the shock of my father's death.

I look at her, down at my own hands and ask, "I beg your pardon?"

"ARE YOU FIRE?"

The question just hangs in the air...

A series of rare events and culminations had convinced us as a family that we were to come to this small, rural area in the deep south of New Zealand. In fact, we were convinced that God was asking us to come to this place. Our work on the surface would be to run an adventure camp. But several prophecies confirmed a personal, but somewhat ambiguous word to me, "Go and ignite!" So we left our family and friends, our home, our community and jobs and set out for the unknown, driven by an unseen fire within our bellies, an unseen energy leading us upwards and onwards. But the tidal waves of life had come fast and furious... leaving us feeling washed up and soaked through.

And here, as I sit like a heap of wet wood in her living room, this woman whom I had never seen before this day has the audacity to ask me, "Are you fire?"

It's a simple, but potent question, saying much more than it asks. The *'Presence'* in it speaks:

51

"Remember who you are and who I AM is! Remember where you draw your energy from."

Remember? Amidst the wind and the waves of life, what have I forgotten? Like Peter, somewhere in the 'stepping out of the boat' onto the 'water,' I have lost sight of Jesus' face.

The Psalmist says, **"He makes his winds messengers, his servant's flames of fire."**[28]

I hear the echo of words I once heard a famous missionary ask running through my head. He asked himself "Am I ignitable?"

Am I?

And maybe more importantly— what if the answer is yes or still wants to be yes, but I find myself soggy damp? Can I be lit?

***

It would not seem so for me this morning.

A deep bone weariness greets me upon waking.

I can feel the intensity of the last two weeks. - So many people, so many needs.

It's 7am and I want to roll back over, hide my head under the pillow and consider spending the day this way.

The demand to keep going is real.

"Mom, we're out of bread" says the one. Another one shouts out, "Yeah and peanut butter and…" and the list goes another 10 items deep. I note a trip to town is needed to stock up.

I stumble into the kitchen, passing the mountain of laundry after a weekend of camp being full of guests, find eggs for breakfast and wish that I liked coffee.

It's Monday. A whole week ahead and my brain swirls in a foggy stupor with one glance at the schedule.

"Mom, I'm sick," croaks another.

---

28 Psalm 104:4

And there goes my day alone.

My hands ache. And I note that my whole body is silently screaming, like the light that flashes red on my car dashboard when fuel levels are dangerously empty.

I reach for the vitamin B tablets. I add in omega 3 and a dose of the evening primrose oil because someone swore that it helped women in their forties adjust to their changing bodies.

I put on my runners to go for my daily spin, trying to think of everything I can be thankful for. After all, "the joy of the Lord is our strength". I open the sliding glass door, push myself out and thank God for the beautiful weather which is not a given for these parts. But truthfully, I just want to lie down. Maybe, I am an ingrate.

"He makes me lie down in green pastures."[29]

I wonder if I'm getting sick.

I quickly chide myself, "Sickness isn't from God." Friends have warned me about making any agreements with the enemy. I rebuke 'sickness.'

But truthfully: I. Still. Just. Want. To. Lie. Down!

"He restores my soul"[30]

I return from a short, stunted walk, switch the jug on for my morning cup of tea and grab my Bible.

I begin to read where I had left off some time before, Luke 6:17: **"Coming down off the mountain with them, he stood on a plain (a level place)."**

Deep calls to deep, before I can finish the first sentence, warm salty wet runs down my cheeks, releasing an unknown, deep cry in my spirit.

O God, could you come down from the heavenly place and meet me at my poor pathetic level? I don't have the strength to climb to you and I am desperate.

---

29 Psalm 23:2a
30 Psalm 23:3

I read on, *"Everyone was trying to touch him—so much energy surging from him, so many people healed! Then he spoke..."*[31]

Once again I hear the quiet whisper of the Presence and am challenged: *"You believe in Jesus of Nazareth! Do you believe He is now? Does He exist only in history? —Someone to respect, believe in and try to follow by your own good works performed for Him? Or is He alive, moving even now, the same energy flowing from Him for all those willing to touch Him?*

I am more of an artist than a scientist, but as I am reading up on energy, I, at the very least, understand that it exists in different forms. I read on, skipping over words like kinetic, mechanical, potential and electrical. I am not sure what revelation I am seeking, but when my eyes see the word "light" something in me lands.

A childhood memory verse repeats itself on my lips as I contemplate these forms of energy: *"In Him was life and that life was the light of men."*[32]

And, I wonder, is it true? Do life and light ultimately exist in a person? Does energy *actually* come from His presence?

If so, all my attempts to gain energy will be like throwing rocks in the waves of the vast Pacific blue. Perhaps, it is I who needs to be thrown in the waves?

But that doesn't make sense. How can you be doused in waves and still have fire?

***

The birds are a symphony outside my window, drawing my eye up and out to a landscape of all sorts of moving shades of green.

The wind and the clouded sun take turns in creating this pattern of dance, while sudden interruptions to its flow flash across my screen; a bumble bee, a will-of-the-wisp looking for a resting place, a bird flying to its nest in the great big pine.

---

31 Luke 6:17 (MSG)
32 John 1:4

Life is teeming outside my window. How is it that most of the time I don't even notice?

When did the roses, cut back to nothing, get this tall? It defied all logic to this amateur when the seasoned gardener said to "cut them right back, as close to the ground as possible!" It felt like murder, not a pruning. But some unspoken, unseen energy has grown their stalks tall, ready to bloom. And I know that this sudden feeling of hope for health, for life, is not just for the roses.

Something like peace begins to settle over me as I feel an unseen rhythm.

My spirit is being made to lie down.

I feel synapses connect in my weary brain and remember this sort of energy afresh.

Something is being restored.

"Are you tired? Worn out? Burned out on religion? Come to me. Get away with me and you'll recover your life. I'll show you how to take a real rest. Walk with me and work with me-watch how I do it. Learn the unforced rhythms of grace."[33]

It is this energy that gave life to that miraculous sound of a tiny heartbeat whooshing inside my swollen abdomen.

And it is this energy that has been morphing my pudgy toddlers' hands into capable almost-men and women hands. I think of all my fears, worries, grasps for control, attempts to be a good parent, to live well and yet some invisible grace is pulling them up towards the sun, like my roses, despite me.

And it is now drawing me.

"T'was Grace that brought us safe thus far and grace will lead us home."[34]

It is this same life force, this invisible grace who commanded "Let there be light!" It is this power that existed before the world, called earth into existence and stuffed itself into the body of Jesus Christ to connect with me personally.

---

33 Matthew 11:28-29 (MSG)
34 William Wilberforce, *Amazing Grace*, 1779

I reread the words of Luke and note that this Messiah didn't puff air, pontificating the meaning of life, expecting us to arise and learn. He demonstrated His love, His energy pulsing towards us, drawing us… before He ever spoke.

And if this is all true, why do we hesitate to run into the arms of the one who can restore us in an instant?

***

The sun is out!

It bursts past the clouds right through my window and warms my face. I feel its effect immediately and yet I cannot see what it looks like on my face.

I look down, my shadow is massive.

Shadows: *dark figures or images cast on the ground or some surface by a body intercepting light[35],* distort our true image. We are too tall, too short, too skinny, too fat. Shadows keep us self-focused vacillating between feeling like we are too much or too little in any given situation.

If I didn't know better, I'd think that perhaps my shadow was really my reflection.

There is a darkness that wants me to think that my shadow is who I am. This darkness weaves around my light, spinning fear, anxiety, doubts, anger, fatigue, insecurities and inadequacies. Its goal: to blindfold and straitjacket all my vigour, zest, zeal and passion. Ultimately, it wants to leave me paralysed.

I shift my focus back to the sun. I can feel the Son beaming down on me, smiling.

A smattering of phrases burst onto the window of my soul:

"If God be for us, who can be against us?"[36]

"There is no condemnation for those who are in Christ Jesus."[37]

---

35 Dictionary.com, 'shadows,' accessed October 12, 2019, https://www.dictionary.com/browse/shadow?s=t
36 Romans 8:31
37 Romans 8:1

"Perfect love casts out fear..."[38]

"Therefore, I will boast all the more gladly about my weaknesses, that Christ's power may rest on me."[39]

This is a God who wants to walk with me not only in my light, but also in my darkness.

***

Maybe that's just it? Maybe we run from God because we don't expect to walk through darkness. We don't expect to see our weaknesses when we say yes to partnering with Him. With God Almighty as our team leader, we expect to always feel victorious. When we don't, we feel as if we are failing, as if we 'should' be doing more, better. Perhaps we are fearful of rejection?

I am not sure what I expected.

The impression of being on fire sounded glorious, it appealed to the wanna-be superhero in me. It flamed a vision of Sarah Almighty walking the streets, singing "I got the power" as I right the world in an instant. No matches needed, just my presence to ignite, arouse and spark. Afterall, didn't the Apostle Peter's very shadow heal people?

But I am beginning to understand that it is not "I, by my will" who will start the fires. Rather, I am to yield my life to the Master as a match.

"What is to give light must endure burning."[40]

I wince when I think of the force and friction that goes into igniting a match.

I ponder all the rubbing up against uncomfortable people, places and things since I have moved overseas.

I hear it again, "Am I ignitable?"

Am I willing to be a match in the hands of the Master?

My heart would say "Yes." But I have a problem. I don't know how to dry out this soggy, damp, bordering-on-mouldy heap.

---

38 1 John 4:18
39 2 Corinthians 12:9
40 Victor Frankl, *The Doctor and the Soul*, 2010

"Nothing is impossible with God."[41]

And it's funny how the *Presence* can make you remember, how it can access and highlight things long shelved.

Jenny Savage, my Sunday school teacher, wore her grey hair pulled back into a low bun. To a ten-year-old, she was not much to look at, but when she told stories about the Bible, she was captivating. She was passionate about the heroes of faith and she made me love the stories too.

I remember her telling us about the mighty prophet Elijah and his massive showdown with the prophets of Baal. Both parties were to build an altar and lay a sacrifice, one in honour of Baal, the other of Jehovah. The God who answered with fire to ignite the sacrifice was the one to be worshipped. The prophets of Baal were disappointed. Elijah, however, built an altar, laid down all the right ingredients and then poured twelve barrels of water over it. Is this the way to see God's glory? Talk about soggy, damp! Elijah prayed:

"O Lord, God of Abraham, Isaac and Israel, let it be known today that you are God ... O Lord, answer me, so these people will know that you, O Lord, are God, and that you are turning their hearts back again."

Then the FIRE of the Lord fell and burned up the sacrifice, the wood, the stones and the soil and licked up the water in the trench. When all the people saw this, they prostrated and cried, **"The Lord—He is God! The Lord—He is God!"**[42]

I am stunned to think of this old story in the context of my present situation. Nothing is impossible with God. If he can do that, certainly my present damp state is not beyond His ignition.

And fire fell from heaven and licked it all up!!!

Maybe life's tidal waves are allowed so that we will cry out, "O Lord, answer me, so that we might know that you, O Lord, are God, and that you are turning our hearts back again!"

The enemy of my soul wants me to think that I am a victim of tragic circumstances. A cruel voice taunts me, tells me to give up, head home.

---

41 Luke 1:37 (MSG)
42 1 Kings 18:36-39

But the Presence reminds me that the stage has only merely been set...

I hear an unseen voice within me say, "Just wait!"

Nothing is impossible with God. For the Lord—He is God! He is God!

rubix cube

an invitation to let God out of the box

"A parable is an allegorical relation of something real. There we have it: a parable deals first of all with Reality. Second, it translates this Reality in terms of imagination. Jesus looked at Reality through the lens of the divine imagination."

-Glen Clark, The Soul's Sincere Desire

In the waiting, darkness seems to have enveloped me.

A stranger in a strange land, fatherless, I am still breathing and with that I recognize that God has not left me. But I can't feel or sense Him anywhere near.

I am puzzled by who God is.

People like to think of Jesus as this man of peace. But he did a lot of stirring. Jesus poked mercilessly at religion. Why am I surprised that He is poking mine? I don't like to think of myself as 'religious.' It seems like a dirty word. But if I am honest, then I have to admit that everyone worships something.

My mind flashes back and I remember a time over a decade ago when I was handed a puzzle to end a dilemma. Why does it seem significant for now?

On that day, I read a sentence on a passing sheet of paper that agitated me so badly I had to go for a walk. I didn't know then that I worshipped my own understanding of things. The phrase simply indicated the idea that *'truth'* has many sides! And yet it socked me fair and square, right in the centre of my evangelical, religious upbringing. I walked furiously fast around the block, trying to understand what had happened. I kept repeating to myself, there aren't many truths, only one truth: Jesus is the way the truth and the life. Mercifully, after a mile, light penetrated my defensive angry gait with a forceful picture in my mind. All my huffing and puffing suddenly dissipated with a vision of a giant Rubix Cube falling to the earth with a thud. Simultaneously I heard, **"I am**

My feet came to a screeching halt as I began to process the vision:

"The Rubix Cube has six different sides and colours that make up its whole. If God is like the Rubix Cube, He is multi-dimensional; he is a chunk of truth, with different sides and colours to be explored."

I waited for the revelation to take its effect. Slowly, I began to grasp that my understanding of God, my defended 'truth' was only a partial truth. The truth itself was greater than I knew. My understanding of God was one dimensional. It was as if I had just picked out one side and one colour of the cube that I had experienced and declared it to be God. As if with great zeal I had declared, "God is yellow!" because I understood, knew and loved the colour yellow. Worse still, I realised that I had so believed in 'yellow' that I was willing to go to bat to protect this understanding, this belief. Isn't that what religion does: require us to defend our group, protect our way?

"Sarah, I don't need you to defend me, I need you to love me. You love me when you love others."

God indeed has a yellow side, but He is far greater than the yellow I limited him to. The music from a recent movie that I watched with my kids, *Prince Caspian*, resounds in my ears. In the film, a lion named Aslan said to the little girl Lucy, "Every year you grow, I grow!" [44]And I wonder if it's *true* that we can't outgrow the Lion of Judah, God himself? –Because it would seem that many of us have tried. Once at a Bible study a woman shared how she had told her husband that she really wanted God to help her with a certain crisis going on in her life. Her husband responded with a penetrating question: "Do you really want His help? Or do you just want God to fix it so that you don't ever really need Him again?"

Ouch.

Do I really expect God to get bigger each time he grows me? Do I anticipate encountering God in different colours, sides and ways? —

---

43 John 14:6
44 *Narnia: Prince Caspian*. DVD. Directed by Andrew Adamson. Burbank: Disney Pictures and Walden Media, 2008

In different denominational lenses, creeds and codes? Do I want to? Am I willing to let God grow out of the box I have for him?

I am reminded of something my father once said and it takes on new context within this discussion: "As you get older, the faith steps just keep on getting bigger." I can't help thinking that those bigger faith steps always require us to move beyond what we know. Paradigm shifts are hard! Perhaps in the days ahead it would be easier for me to think of the changes I am encountering, not as leaving behind the people I love, places I adore or even the 'Truths' I have learned. Perhaps I may embrace a notion that I am being added to, expanding, crossing into new dimensions and colours of the person of God. Perhaps, the Truth, the Way and the Life is calling me to discover new dimensions and colours?

I wonder, what does that look like?

"And I pray that you, being rooted and established in love, may have power, together with all the Lord's holy people, to grasp how wide and long and high and deep is the love of Christ, and to know this love that surpasses knowledge—that you may be filled to the measure of all the fullness of God."[45]

There is a beautiful invitation before me to explore God in all His greatness, in all His love—an invitation that passes religion. Just knowing God in one dimension is not enough. This is an appeal to be led beyond my present coloured square to a new colour, that I *might be filled to the measure of all the fullness of God.*

Strangely encouraged, two questions then beg to be asked: What is it about this Rubix Cube memory that is pertinent for me to remember now in my waiting? And if God is truly like a Rubix Cube, where would I place myself in or on the cube?

As I ponder this, I can't help but wonder that if God wanted to move me in my understanding from one side, colour or way of understanding to the complete opposite side, to encounter yet another dimension of Himself, would I not find myself in Antipodes?

Bingo! Indeed, this past memory is pertinent to now.

---

45 Ephesians 3:17b-19

I contemplate the routes that I could take if I were on the cube; up and over, down and over, around and across. But the fastest way to get to the opposite side—right through the centre! If in this analogy God is the entire cube, then wouldn't the centre be the very heart of God himself? I imagine what the inside of a cube might seem like; wouldn't it be dark, black, maybe even claustrophobic? At the very least, wouldn't the sudden stillness, lack of colour and quiet be foreign?

"He who dwells in the shelter of the Most High will rest in the shadow of the Almighty. I will say of the Lord, 'He is my refuge and my fortress, my God, in whom I trust.'"[46]

The concept works its way from my head into the depths of my soul. I think of the black emptiness that I have felt all around me as I wait for grief to finish its way in me. And part of the grief in it all has been that God seems unrecognisable. Suddenly, I realize that this strange darkness I find myself in may not be the evil I supposed. Rather, what if it is actually the very heart of God himself; where He is holding me, carrying me through to the other side?

"Surely the darkness will hide me, and the light become night around me, even the darkness will not be dark to you, the night will shine like the day, for darkness is as light to you."[47]

It has felt like I have been sinking down into an abyss. What if I have been swept up into the core of God himself? This then must be a waiting room with a purpose that is yet to be defined. The truth that I can hold onto is that I am not alone and that God knows exactly where we are going.

As I think about this, I realize that I have understood this in theory since I was a child and read the poem, *Footprints*, on my friend's bathroom wall.

I suspect that this theory is about to be refined and substantiated by a teacher named Experience. What will it look like for this truth to be forged into the very core of my being?

Once again, I yield as I read:

---

46 Psalm 91:1
47 Psalm 139:11-12

He whispered,

"My precious child, I love you and will never leave you
Never, ever, during your trials and testings,
When you saw only one set of footprints,
It was then that I carried you."[48]

---

48 Author Unknown, *Footprints in the Sand.*

positioned

an invitation to be made authentic

"The words printed here are concepts. You must go through the experiences."

-St Augustine

This invitation to allow theories to be transformed by experience sounds easy.

A-Z is easy enough to write. But there are a lot of letters that go on in between.

Somehow, something in me recognizes that to continue to sojourn in Antipodes, I will need courage; courage to journey with God into the desolate internal landscape of my soul and courage to fight an invisible battle.

In theory, I understand that the battle is really an ancient lie that began in a garden. I don't think the enemy of our souls is that creative. The lie spoken in Eden is repeated again and again: *"God's not good! He's holding out on you! Why even bother?"* But I'm finding in the blackness, in the longing, it can almost seem believable.

Can I resist the lie that tells me that I have landed in a pit, not in the Shelter of the Most High?

In theory, I understand that I will need audacity to face God in a way that is outside of the box, outside of how I am comfortable thinking of him. It is not an easy task to be asked to: "let go!" I will have to let go of certain notions to be open to encountering God in new ways and I will have to have trust that He is indeed bigger, much bigger than I ever imagined. This makes me nervous; in practice, I fear that having to stretch beyond the boxes I have made for faith, for God, will feel much like childbirth. As a mother of four children, I know what goes into a birth. Will I have strength to endure the contracting and expanding of my soul? How long will this labour be before I get to the point of exhaustion—of, "I JUST CAN'T DO THIS ANYMORE!?" And what will be birthed?

"So be strong and courageous. Do not be terrified; do not be discouraged, for the Lord your God will be with you wherever you go."[49]

Our family takes a day to explore the small city of Dunedin. It feels like a massive metropolitan area after being in farm country. We all seem to be sighing with relief upon the re-entry into what we consider civilization. Although it is not a massive city, its old world charm by the bay promises a diversity of flavours in food, people and thought. Most importantly, it has a Starbucks Café, promising everyone a taste of home. Everyone is discussing what they want to order as we file in. Before I know what hits me, I find myself back outside on the street, weeping uncontrollably. I wasn't prepared; I had no idea what just the smell of the place could do. I am not a coffee drinker, but my father was, he loved his Starbucks decaf grande. I had no idea that this smell of home would generate a tidal wave of grief. Sometimes these waves come out of nowhere, when least expected, leaving me uncomfortably undone.

I gather myself together and order a classic hot chocolate with whipped cream. We bask in the taste of the familiar before we meander in and out of the shops on the main strip and end up at the Octagon in the Art Museum. There are paintings, sculptures; some colourful, some bold, some quiet…all ministering to our souls in different ways. But it's a group of words written on the wall that arrests my attention. Surrounding the words are a group of New Zealand landscape paintings for effect:

"If You Don't Know Where You Are, You Don't Know Who You Are."

The effect is not lost on me. The words create a temporary shelter of understanding for this lost and weary traveller. I don't know this landscape of the soul. I don't know where home is. And truthfully, I am not sure I know myself as I once thought I did.

I feel vulnerable.

Part of the courage required is to admit just that, and it makes my head spin. I have been trained to always put my best foot forward, to be professional, to put on a game face. But I can feel the ultimate dare of this journey is to take off my masks and be made real.

---

49 Joshua 1:9

"I will boast of the things that show my weaknesses."[50]

I am being asked to admit that I don't have it all together. I am being asked to confess that I have questions; more questions than answers.

It totally goes against my grain: the sudden outbursts of tears that grief brings. I don't like feeling weak, especially in this deep South land, settled by the Scots. The Scottish heritage seems to have an unspoken, forbidden rule against weeping. They are strong, independent people who know how to "pull themselves up by their bootstraps'. In addition (if my overgeneralization of an entire people group is not enough), it should be mentioned that I do live in a small town. Small towns don't breed vulnerability. There is something inherently unsafe if one is found exposed, unguarded. People talk. And moreover, it's a conservative town. In short, there are many who like their boxes. It will take courage to be someone who ponders and asks honest questions, especially ones that might pierce established orders of religion in the ways around us.

By nature, I am not bold, or audacious, or daring. I feel slightly faint at what I will need to become to survive the new land.

How O God, does this work?

How do I navigate this strange upside-down land of the heart? How do I find my way through Antipodes?

Do you have any instructions for where I have landed?

IS THERE A MAP?

My eyes land on Jesus words to his disciples in the book of Luke and they resound within me:

> ***"Blessed are you who are poor,***
> ***for yours is the kingdom of God.***
> ***Blessed are you who hunger now,***
> ***for you will be satisfied.***
> ***Blessed are you who weep now,***
> ***for you will laugh.***

---

50 2 Corinthians 11:30

Blessed are you when people hate you,
when they exclude you and insult you
and reject your name as evil, for my name's sake.[51]

What?

Is this the map?

I look up the Greek word for blessed. The Greek word is *Makarios*[52] and it means for one to be supremely blessed, fortunate and/or well off.

Huh???

This is not the message I get from the world all around me. Poverty, hunger, weeping and persecution are generally not desirable. They are not thought of as an enviable position to be in to receive God's favour and grace in some larger, greater way.

Jesus's words reveal a different value system. In fact, it seems to be completely upside down from this world I live in. He seems to delight in and promise to show himself to the poor, satisfy the hungry, give joy to the hurting and applause to the persecuted.

Do I want to be blessed like this?

This is an upside-down, antipodean, if you will, way of thinking.

Is it possible that in this upside-down place I have found myself, I am being positioned to encounter God's kingdom right-side up?

One commentary said that to be blessed this way is to be "one who has become a partaker of God; *and/or one who* experiences the fullness of God."[53]

Perhaps this present state of being turned inside out and upside-down is not only an invitation to travel into the very heart of God himself, but also to step into the darkness, the upside-down experience of what makes God's heartbeat wildly.

---

51 Luke 6:20b-22 (MSG)
52 Greek: 3107. μακάριος (Makarios) -- blessed, happy. Accessed October 12, 2019. https://www.biblehub.com/greek/3107.htm.
53 Studylight.org, 'Makarios,' accessed October 14, 2019, https://www.studylight.org/language-studies/greek-thoughts.html?article=38

What if the desolate landscape to traverse is my own poverty, hunger, negative emotions and fear of people turning against me? And no sooner do I ask this, then I know that it is the path being laid before me. I consider running, giving up on my faith. I could just live a quiet life tucked away in the backwoods somewhere. Then Jesus' words leap from the pages of the book of Mark: *"Anyone who intends to come with me has to let me lead. You're not in the driver's seat; I am. Don't run from suffering, embrace it. Follow me and I'll show you how. Self-help is no help at all. Self-sacrifice is the way, my way, to saving yourself, your true self. What good would it do to get everything you want and lose you? What could you ever trade your soul for?"[54]*

Suddenly, I relate to the princess from the movie Enchanted[55], who falls from Happily- Ever- After Land to New York City. Before she emerges, she finds herself in a black space where she begins to transform from something animated to real.

Maybe we are all like this?

Maybe this is what happens when time is spent in the centre of the cube, in the depths of God's heart. Here, the fake, the phony is rubbed off. The heart is freed to move in time with God's heartbeat where His rhythm can pump the blood and oxygen I so desperately need through my veins…

---

54 Mark 8:34-37 (MSG)
55 Adams. Amy. *Enchanted*. DVD. Directed by Kevin Lima. Burbank, Walt Disney Motion Pictures, 2007

tidal wave
an invitation to move within the source of life

"It came down like a tidal wave, sorrow swept over me."

-Owl City

My new darkness of soul breeds a weird kind of loneliness. Not only have I not felt the nearness of God, but when I went to church, I felt odd. I felt disconnected from the people and I could not embrace what the preacher said.   -

The preacher meant well.

A straightforward, no-frills kind of man, he challenged us to lift our eyes from the waves and put them back on Jesus.

I know this story well.

It seems to have been a favourite subject for many a sermon I have heard in my years: Impetuous Peter, willing to risk the impossible at the Lord's bidding, steps out of the boat, when suddenly he is overwhelmed by the opposition of stormy waves and begins to sink into the deep. As his body begins to descend, he cries out to the Lord to save him. Immediately, Jesus catches him and says, "You of little faith, why did you doubt?"

I always imagined Peter on the water, just beginning to sink, when he lifts his eyes to the Lord.

My understanding? Jesus was somewhere within Peter's view. *Surely there is a time to relinquish doubt and keep our eyes on the Lord.*

But what if I find myself already submerged in the water with a 30-foot tidal wave looming above me, blocking off the sight of sky, let alone the Lord's face?

"...you have overwhelmed me with all your waves."[56]

---

56 Psalm 88:7b

70

What if I call to the Lord and there seems to be no answer, just the wave crashing over me, tumbling me in the deep? Am I the only one to have ever asked this question? It feels almost sacrilegious, but the questions keep coming…

Has someone failed?

Me? If only I had somehow grabbed hold of God's hand, had more faith?

God? My rock, my shield, my strong deliverer?

Or worse, what if it's all a farce?

And yet, there before me are the first words that Jesus spoke after letting his 'energy' surge and heal others, stopping me in my tracks: ***"Blessed are you who are poor, for yours is the kingdom of God."***[57]

I confess. I have heard this 'beatitude' a thousand times and never really thought much of it. "Okay, so God likes poor people" is about where it has landed in me. I read its counterpoint verse: ***"But woe to you who are rich, for you have already received your comfort."*** Yikes! I begin to think of all the people I know who are 'poor'— *who should I be helping?* Clearly, it's an incredible ideal, caring for the poor and I 'should' try to live my life accordingly. How? I find myself asking, "What does this really mean? Does it have any bearing for me, besides some feeling that I should sponsor another child in Africa?"

So, I reread the words in another version: ***"You're blessed when you've lost it all. God's kingdom is there for the finding."*** Now, something cracks when I read the words. I reread them again, counter verse included: ***"But it's trouble ahead if you think you have it made. What you have is all you'll ever get."***[58]

I mutter to the air, "What is cracking, God?"

I wasn't expecting an answer, He's been silent for so long. My heart jumps when I hear a response:

"Your bubble of idealism."

---

57 Luke 6:20
58 Luke 6:24

I clarify what is meant by *'idealism'* on the online dictionary: *The tendency to represent things in an ideal form, or as they might or should be rather than as they are, with emphasis on values.*[59]

Do I believe that I or my life should be something other than it is?

"...You are blessed when you have lost it all."[60]

Certainly, the world does not celebrate *losing it all.* It's rarely a good thing to fall apart. But clearly, the kind eyes from heaven are blessing those who are poor and the poor in spirit. They are blessing those who have nothing and those who are swirling and twirling, thrashing and crashing in the deep, blessing those who don't know which way is up. And suddenly those same eyes turn and look at me...and for just a moment I can feel my pride wanting to protest against the implication.

Heaven's kind eyes turn towards me, flames of fire that burn right through my barriers, ideals, knowledge and intellect. Suddenly, I am aware of how hard I have been trying to understand the big picture of the emotional landscape I stand in. As I dare to look, I note that the flames in His eyes become *deep pools*. After all this time, God is present; His *deep pools* of empathy find their way to my eyes. As I let my gaze linger there, I can feel my lip and chin begin to tremor. My own pain, questions and doubts are being reflected back to me in His eyes. He knows, He sees and I come face to face with my own poverty.

Having a degree in Social Work, I am aware that 'the poor' often cannot end their own misery; I am being invited to admit my inner reality— I am poor and can't get out of this on my own. At the end of the day, all my positive thinking, self-help techniques, "pull myself up by the bootstraps" attempts, cannot remove the black sediment that, when provoked, begins to swirl in my deep. Jesus is not just a good thought, a good way...the profound truth is that I need Him, like a new-born who needs her mama. *"I am the way, the truth, the life,"*[61] is not a mere ideological, dogmatic, religious statement on how to get to heaven; it is an appeal to move within the source of life.

---

59 Dictionary.com, 'Idealism,' accessed October 12, 2019, https://www.dictionary.com/browse/idealism?s=t
60 Luke 6:20 (MSG)
61 John 14:6

I search the eyes of *deep pools*, knowing instinctively that it is okay to say it, even with doubt in my voice. Still, I feel some reluctance and realize that my ideals have kept me from asking it before now. Like Martha, I have stood resolute in my understanding, in my trust:

"Lord had you been here, my brother would have not died. But I know that even now God will give you whatever you ask."[62]

"I am the resurrection and the life." [63]

Like Martha, my trust has been rewarded with more knowledge of Himself. He has stayed with me right where I am, giving me bits of Himself, bits of understanding as I am ready. I think of the Rubix Cube analogy, the Antipodean map— bits of understanding that I am holding unto; yes, like Martha, I have sought to understand. I have made myself dizzy some days trying to understand.

Martha's sister is Mary. I used to think she was weak. Mary says the exact same thing as her sister, but without a faith follow-up statement, without strength or even seemingly trust: *"Lord had you been here, my brother would not have died."[64]* Only her tears and brokenness are evident. But today as I look at this story, something is shifting within me; maybe, just maybe, Mary was the strong one. Perhaps it takes greater strength to let a tear roll down her cheek, admitting her brokenness, questions and deep need. For Jesus doesn't chide her: *"O, you of little faith,"[65]* he meets her emotion with his own.

Mary's brave honesty *moves* the heart of God to act. *"Where have they laid him?"[66]*

God is not callous, aloof to our needs: *"The Lord is gracious and compassionate, slow to anger and rich in love."[67]*

Am I honest with God in such a way that I *move* him?

---

62 John 11:21
63 John 11:25
64 John 11:32
65 Luke 12:287
66 John 11:34
67 Psalm 145:8

Eyes of compassion meet me in my own poverty, my own pain and I finally blurt it out— *"Lord, had you been here, my father would not have died!"* It's then that I see tears run from Jesus' eyes; He weeps with me. And I am comforted in a way that theology and mental understanding can't bring; He validates my humanity.

I think of the 'Sarah Almighty' who envisioned her shadow healing people, coming to help 'ignite' a nation. I didn't realize that if I wanted to see the dead rise , I would find myself on my knees, surrendering all my understanding and experiencing my own brokenness. Is suffering not the prerequisite for resurrection power?

Jesus turns to me as he did the sisters and says, ***"Did I not tell you that if you believed that you would see the glory of God?"*[68]**

I ask again: What kind of glory? My father's ashes have been engulfed by the Pacific. I don't expect my father to be resurrected after all these months.

Heaven's kind eyes meet mine again. Deep pools of empathy enlighten my poverty. It is not my father who needs answers, who needs life— it's me! Suddenly, like a wounded dog, I snap: *"Where were you? It's lovely to see your eyes in this moment, but where were you when the tidal waves came? When I expected to see your face, to take your hand and instead found myself plunged into the watery deep, the abyss?"*

***"Deep calls to deep in the roar of your waterfalls; all your waves and breakers have swept over me."*[69]**

Deep calls to deep. I love the thought of the depth of God calling out to mine. Still, it doesn't answer my question—where have you been? I pick up my Bible and find the verse to read it fresh; it's then that my eyes fixate on the tiny little preposition word "*in.*" I am stunned! The Deep, The Presence calls to us *in* the waves and breakers, in the tumbling, swirling and thrashing. ***"Never will I leave you, nor forsake you!"*[70]** I expected God's righteous right arm to save me, to pull me up out of the waves. It felt like in my greatest hour of need, He had abandoned me; but all this time He has been hovering.

---

68 John 11:40
69 Psalm 42:7
70 Hebrews 13:5b

'Hovering' is an interesting word to write and I find myself curious to its existence, if at all, in the Bible. I look up the word in the Bible concordance and discover it is first used in Genesis 1:2: *"Now the earth was formless and empty, darkness was over the surface of the deep, and the spirit of God was hovering over the waters."*

Does the creation of the world have anything to do with my present state?

I check online for the Hebrew word for hovering; it is *'rachaph.'*[71] It means to relax, flutter, move and shake. I find it interesting to note that as God is hovering over the world, he is not anxious or worried. There is movement, fluttering and shaking, but without urgency, drama, angst, fear, or anger. I like the words that the online bible tool uses to describe God's hovering; 'to grow soft; relax'. For some reason, it makes me remember my mother teaching me how to relax, breathe slowly, sway gently with my agitated newborn. She said, "Babies can feed off what they are feeling from you. If you are agitated, they will cry more. But if you are calm, it will calm them."

With that thought, oddly Jesus's words, *"Let not your heart be troubled, trust in God, trust also in me,"*[72] run through my mind; honestly, I have always felt like they were a bit of an unrealistic command. But if God is relaxed, like a mama soothing her flailing newborn baby, cooing, *'It's okay, Mama's got you;'* Jesus' words take on a whole new meaning. The words aren't meant to make us try harder, but rather, to relax into Him. Even now, could Jesus be trying to comfort me? Is he holding me, swaying with me, saying *"Shush-shush, honey…I've got this"*? Do I want to relax into him?

I note a second verse in which *rachaph* is used: *"In a desert land he found him, in a barren and howling waste. He shielded him and cared for him: he guarded him as the apple of his eye, like an eagle that stirs up its nest, that hovers over its young, He spread His wings and caught them, He carried them on His pinions."* [73]

I have heard how eagles stir up their nest, how they begin to remove the softness so that the eaglets will want to leave and become self-

71 Bibletools.org, 'Rachaph,' accessed October 14, 2019, https://www.bibletools.org/index.cfm/fuseaction/Lexicon.show/ID/H7363/rachaph.htm
72 John 14:1
73 Deuteronomy 32:10-11

sufficient adults. Does God want to train me, mature me? I flashback and remember trying to teach my firstborn to take a nap. I would lay her down awake in her crib when she was tired; making sure that she had had every possible need met before walking out the door and standing just on the other side to listen. Initially she would cry and after a few minutes I would go back in and reassure her, then once again, I would stand just outside the door and wait. Slowly she learned that her naps were good for her, safe and that I would never leave her. She learned to feel secure in her own bed and with her own company; she learned to not be afraid if I was out of her sight, because Mama was there when she woke up. And with that memory, I understand that after all this time, God has been here with me; maybe not in my vision, but nearby, watching and waiting.

"There is an appointed time for everything under heaven."[74]

Apparently there is a time to believe and reach for the hand of God and there is also a time to submit to the waves and trust that some far deeper work is at hand. The Hebrew word for deep is *'tehom.'*[75] Why am I not surprised that it also means 'sea or abyss?' And somehow it does not seem to be coincidental that the first place it is used is in Genesis 1:2: ***"Now the earth was formless and empty, darkness was over the surface of the deep (tehom) and the Spirit of God was hovering over the waters."[76]***

I muse that it was as if the earth was not yet energised. Suddenly, I understand how my circumstances relate to creation: Have I not been crying out for energy? And like the prehistoric earth, there are parts of my heart terrain that are dark, without form, without motion, without light…

I read a bit more from the commentary and note that light, a form of energy, was not yet present: ***"…the whole was shrouded in the thick folds of Cimmerian gloom, giving not the slightest promise of that fair world of light, order and life into which it was about to be transformed. Only one spark of hope might have been detected in the circumstance that the Spirit of God moved (literally, brooding) upon the face of the waters."[77]***

---

74 Ecclesiastes 3:1
75 Biblehub.com, 'Genesis 1:2,' accessed October 14, 2019, https://biblehub.com/hebrew/8415.htm
76 Genesis 1:1-2
77 Studylight.org, 'Genesis 1:2,' accessed October 14, 2019, https://www.studylight.org/commentaries/tpc/genesis-1.html9

I feel anticipation rise within me when I read that the Spirit of God, the *ruach*, literally translates to *wind*, or *breath,* was hovering over the waters.[78] Hovering... undulating... moving... quaking... shaking... vibrating —wouldn't all that motion create friction, like heat generated from hands rubbed back and forth together quickly? I think of the 'friction' that has been created in me within the waves of life, in the tumbling, swirling and thrashing. I think of the friction needed to light a match and I am in awe of how things come full circle; for there before me are God's first recorded words... *"Let. There. Be. Light!"*[79]

Ignition!-'Ex Nihilo'[80], ***Out of nothing*** the Spirit brought illumination and energy, light and life.

I feel a drop of hope penetrate my heart. Not only does God want to walk with me in my blackout, He is a specialist in making light out of darkness, form out of void and energy out of that which is motionless. Moreover, He is completely relaxed, His heart soft to my present state.

I consider Jesus' words again: ***"You are blessed when you have lost it all. God's kingdom is there for the finding."***[81]

I hear the Lord unpack that verse at my level: *Happy are those who have nothing, who have lost it all, who feel broken and know their own poverty for they have been given a front row seat to witness the God of all creation work miracles, to transform their darkness into light and their nothingness into burgeoning life.*

His kind eyes look at me again; this time they reflect the memory of riding on the tractor with my daddy. I am being invited to climb up into God's lap; trust that His hands are on the wheel alongside mine and to rest in his safety and security.

I hesitate. There is a part of me that wants to, but if I am honest, there are still so many questions in the way. Some part of me is flailing within, just wanting to go home. When I imagine this part of me, I am humbled by the image of a colicky baby wanting to be soothed, but in too much pain to be so. I want to respond to God's comfort, but there is still too much 'gas' within me. I have not digested whatever I have

78 Biblehub.com, 'Genesis 1:2,' accessed October 14, 2019, https://biblehub.com/hebrew/7307.htm
79 Luke 6:20
80 Wikipedia.com, Ex-Nihilo, accessed May 23, 2020, https://en.m.wikipedia.org
81 Luke 6:20

absorbed thus far in Antipodes well enough, perhaps my system needs time to mature like one of these newborns?

God doesn't seem to flinch at my hesitation, instead, he puts out his hand for me to take, as if to go for a stroll. I understand that he'll take this slowly; *he will shield me and care for me; he will guard me as the 'apple of his eye,' and he will give me the time I need to adjust. Then* I suspect *he will stir up the nest,* nudging me towards maturity.

home

an invitation to be anchored by the great love of the ancient one

"The journey homewards. Coming home. That's what it's all about. The journey and the coming of the kingdom. That's probably the chief difference between the Christian and secular artist—the purpose of the work, be it story or music or painting, is to further the coming of the kingdom, to make us aware of our status of children of God, and to turn our feet toward home."
-Madeleine l'Engle

Where the Presence hovers, order and life begin.

Suddenly the morning's madness takes focus.

I had struggled to get out of bed, fighting off some invisible blackness. And apparently, I was not the only one feeling the heaviness. My ears awoke to whines, grumbles, bickering, even swearing. My children are on the bus and I, my walk, before I can finally process what in the world is going on.

"O Lord! What is happening? What is this?"

His simple reply was: *"It's February 17th, 2013."*

It's February 17th. Memory overwhelms me with a smattering of smells, places, words and embraces that signify my father's being. I almost reach for the phone, wondering if I can get him at this moment. Will I get him, be able to wish him a happy birthday, or will it just be his machine?

I contemplate his serious, almost impersonal answering machine message:

"This is RE Howe; I am not available at the moment. If you would please leave your name and phone number, I will try to get back to you as quickly as possible."

How many times have I heard that message and rolled my eyes? That's not the real man. I wondered how many who did not really know him might have thought him cool, even calculated? It is quite a contrast to how he would greet me, his eldest daughter, especially after we moved overseas. Always a lull on the long distant line, hope and joy brimming, ready to burst with his greeting, "Is this my girl, calling all the way from New Zealand???"

Some part of my heart would leap as I answered yes. *"O yes, yes it's me... your girl."*

And in an instant, I'd feel anchored, wrapped up. *I am loved. I am known. I belong.*

Something more than tears seem to be falling as I realize there will be no phone calls this year. And I feel a strange ripping all over again of the Velcro that held my heart with Dad's. He is gone, 'passed away'— but that term doesn't quite seem to cut what I bore witness to. Two months into his terminal illness, Dad said, "I've been thinking that if I'm really going to die, I am going to have to shed this mortal body so that my spirit can go. That means I will feel some pain. I don't really want to feel pain, but I realize pain is a good thing as it will help me to release all that I want to hold onto here. It will help make me ready to leave." I think his pain made us all want to release him. But, nonetheless, it's a trauma to watch someone beloved shed their body within five months.

They say time is a healer. Certainly, the waves have come further apart with less intensity. But today, his birthday, a storm threatens to rock me to my core and I …

I surrender.

"Deep calls to deep in the roar of your waterfalls; all your waves and breakers have swept over me."[82]

Have I not been learning that there is a time to be still and let God work in the dark places?

"By day the Lord directs his love, at night his song is with me— a prayer to the God of my life."[83]

---

82 Psalm 42:7
83 Psalm 42:8

I wonder about this night song. And note what follows:

"I say to God my Rock, "Why have you forgotten me? Why must I go about mourning, oppressed by the enemy?" My bones suffer mortal agony as my foes taunt me, saying to me all day long, "Where is your God?"[84]

I had just been complaining yesterday that my bones ached. How many times have I thought that I might have some disease when it is only my grief demanding an audience with God?

"Why are you downcast, O my soul? Why so disturbed within me? Put your hope in God, for I will yet praise him, my Saviour and my God."[85]

Is it possible that my soul can grieve, question, even doubt, while my spirit leads me to say there is still hope, put it in God?

I remember an old book I once read, I race upstairs, find it dusty on the shelf. And there in it, written nearly six hundred years earlier, lies an excerpt from the writings of St. John of the Cross called <u>The Dark Night of The Soul</u>.

"God perceives the imperfections within us and because of his love for us, urges us to grow up. His love is not content to leave us in our weakness and for this reason he takes us into a dark night. He weans us from all of the pleasures by giving us dry times and inward darkness....

Through the dark night pride becomes humility, greed becomes simplicity, wrath becomes contentment, luxury becomes peace, gluttony becomes moderation, envy becomes joy and sloth becomes strength. No soul will ever grow deep in the spiritual life unless God works passively in that soul by means of the dark night."[86]

And my spirit understands that the dousing and tumbling among the waves I am engulfed in are not without purpose. Perhaps it is in this dark night that my soul is being purified and my spirit is being matured and strengthened to lead.

---

84 Psalm 42:9-10
85 Psalm 51:7-12
86 Foster & Smith, *Devotional Classics*, (San Francisco, Harper, 1990), p.36

81

"Cleanse me with hyssop, and I will be clean; wash me, and I will be whiter than snow. Let me hear joy and gladness; let the bones you have crushed rejoice. Hide your face from my sins and blot out all my iniquity. Create in me a pure heart, O God, and renew a steadfast spirit within me. Do not cast me from your presence or take your Holy Spirit from me. Restore to me the joy of your salvation and grant me a willing spirit to sustain me."[87]

Something like hope rises within me again: My spirit is anchored by the great love of the Ancient One. *I am loved. I am known. I belong.*

I understand that I am His girl. He meets me in the waves, washing over me with His love.

I heard it once said as a rebuke to another, *"To despair is to turn your back on God."* To despair is to lose all hope. It is to find yourself at the bottom of a pit, utterly hopeless. How many of us have felt like we were 'bad' for even feeling hopelessness? But now I know that even the depths of despair cannot keep Him away.

Deep calls to deep!

***

I say it to myself again. It's February 17th.

But this time there is a bit of debate in my head. Maybe, I am premature in my grief.

Actually, it's Monday, nearing 10am on February 17th here today, down under. The season is about to change from summer to autumn. However, there, on the West Coast of America, in this exact moment, it is Sunday, nearing 1pm on February 16th. The season is also changing, only from winter to spring.

I want to call my mother, my sister, my brother. But I realize that they are not yet feeling this moment; I am ahead of them in time. I long to go to them, hug them when I have a sudden strange thought: Can my prayers today on the 17th make way for them to enter their 17th tomorrow?

---

87 Psalm 51:7-12

"Praise be to the God and Father of our Lord Jesus Christ, the Father of compassion and the God of all comfort, who comforts us in all our troubles, so that we can comfort those in any trouble with the comfort we ourselves have received from God."[88]

Here's an even more wild thought: If this moment in time can be rightly called both winter and summer, the 16th and the 17th, 10am and 1am depending on one's perspective, then what do they call this moment where Dad is standing? For I am convinced that as certain as the northern and southern hemispheres co-exist in time, there is yet another sphere that I have not yet encountered that operates alongside us, outside of us, or above us?

I know this because *The Presence that Calls to Me with Love* whispers that I am loved, known and belong. I know my father knew this Presence. *"And I am convinced that neither death nor life, neither angels nor demons, neither the present nor the future, nor any powers, neither height nor depth, nor anything else in all creation, will be able to separate us from the love of God, that is in Christ Jesus our Lord."*[89]

I don't know the season, the day or the year of where Dad is; I can't call him. But I know the Saviour, I know Love and I know Dad is with him. What if Dad has gone ahead to this sphere that I call heaven to intercede on our behalf; to make way for us to join him?

"Since we are surrounded by such a great cloud of witnesses, let us throw off everything that hinders and the sin that so easily entangles, and let us run with perseverance the race marked out for us. Let us fix our eyes on Jesus, the author and perfecter of our faith."[90]

***

It's just a picture of an empty bench sitting on a cliff overlooking the ocean with this caption: "If you could have just one hour with any person dead or alive, who would you want to speak with?" Some lump catches in my throat and my heart fills with longing for moments gone by sitting on a bench just like that with my father just outside of his

---

88 2 Corinthians 1:3-4
89 Romans 8:38-39
90 Hebrews 12:1

home in Shell Beach. How I wish I could ask his advice on all that is happening now.

Loss overwhelms me, "Lord?"

Immediately I see His eyes looking deeply into mine. They are pools again, deep pools, and as I look back into them, I see the pools turn into oceans. Quite suddenly I can see in my mind's eye the house that was my parent's home at the beach in California. And somehow, I understand that home is in His eyes. Home is in him.

It's all in HIM. The northern and southern hemispheres, the oceans, even life and death. That which belongs to Him is eternal, joined, connected.

My living family is not as far away as I think. My father is even closer. All I need to do is look into my Saviour's eyes and I will know again that what has been forged in eternity can never be separated.

In His eyes, I find myself again. I find stability. I find home.

"Blessed are you who are poor for yours is the kingdom of God."[91]

I feel a strange relief in knowing that when I am poor, He is rich, and when I am weak, He is strong. I may only be at the beginning of my upside-down journey through Antipodes, but I know that I am not alone, he has taken my hand and with that I turn to face the unknown journey before me.

Just before I leave, I see the picture of the bench again. I still miss my father. But I look back at those eyes with Deep Pools in them, draw hope and whisper:

"Lord, would you please tell my father "Happy Birthday!"

---

91 Luke 6:20

hun.ger

1. a compelling need or desire for food.
2. the painful sensation or state of weakness caused by the need of food
3. a shortage of food; famine.
4. a strong or compelling desire or craving.

"Blessed are you who hunger now,
for you will be satisfied."
Luke 6:21

AFTERMATH YEAR TWO:
IF GOD CAN, WHY DOESN'T HE?

---

thirst
an invitation into the passion of Christ

"Love is a thirst—a need as vital to the soul as water is to the body."

-Colleen Houck

In the province of Poverty, I felt all my ideals begin to crack, making way for something far grittier: authenticity.

Discovering my own poverty and the nearness of God in it has made me curious to learn more about the strange upside-down instructions Jesus gives in Luke chapter six. When Jesus blesses the poor, the hungry, the weeping and the persecuted, He is not praising different types of people going through different things in different parts of the world. But rather He is blessing one kind of person, the kind of person who is willing *to be made* poor, hungry, sad and persecuted in order to see God.

I am not sure where I acquired an unspoken belief that Christians shouldn't ever feel sadness, doubt, hurt, anxiety, depression or even fear. But clearly, I have been wrong. Jesus doesn't seem to be disappointed by these human emotions. Rather God not only seems to be right here as promised but is offering to be my home away from home as I traverse Antipodes.

If that's the case, I've only begun this journey. I am understanding that embracing my own poverty is just the invite to encounter God in the rest of my darkness. The cracking apart of all my ideals has made way for the doubts, questions, apathy and pride to be examined. I consider running away again. I could say, "No thanks, God. I think we are good. I'll just cross this place by myself. I think I can take it from here." But for now, I must admit that curiosity wins.

I note that the word courage comes from the French word *"coeur"* which translates "heart."[92] Hence, a courageous person is one who chooses to live with heart. Does anyone not want to live with heart?

92 Dictionary.com, 'Courage,' accessed Oct 12, 2019, https://www.dictionary.com/browse/courage?s=t

I resolve to gather my heart and move forward towards him. I want more of Jesus. I have had a taste of the kind of love that can expel fear and I am hungry for more.

I spoke with a dear friend about things here in Southland. And she said, "It sounds like you are acclimating not only to the temperature but also to the people, the culture."

Southland is thirsty now.

We are going on five weeks without rain this summer and I hear the word 'drought' whispered with a tone of fear among the farmers and their wives. It seems strange to this girl from the golden hills of California that these greenish hills would be declaring a drought already.

But everything depends on the weather here. They do not have the irrigation system that California does. They rely on rain falling from heaven.

And as I write this, to my delight, a light rain begins.

Water from heaven spits promises into the drought of this great Southern land and I wonder if there might be enough to moisten the dryness in the back land of my throat.

"Do not be afraid…For I will pour water on the thirsty land, and streams on the dry ground."[93]

Do not be afraid? Am I afraid of something in this season of personal drought?

I survey the land outside my windows and wonder what it would be like for heaven's rain to penetrate the ground of hearts.

Before I came here, I asked God, "Why am I going to New Zealand?"

Immediately I saw a picture of Google Earth. It was as if God was hovering over the globe waiting to reveal the address typed in. Instead of an address, a question was typed in, *"Are you out there, God? —Are you really, really out there?"* And then as the globe turned, I could see a presence moving in towards New Zealand, it moved to the very bottom of the island, zeroed in on a house, went in and stood before a person momentarily, before it took the liberty of moving inside of the person.

---

93 Isaiah 44:2-3

It would seem now, that my cry has joined the deep cry of hearts here, *"Are you out there, God? Are you really, really out there? Come to me, come move within me. Come to us, come move within us…"*

My eyes shift inside and linger on the old wooden cutting board. It's been used, washed clean, used and washed clean, again and again. And even though it's clean, it's cracking.

I think of all the *faithful* souls I have met here in Southland, New Zealand.

These saints serve the best they know how. They too know what it is to be used and washed clean. Here they are not a people given to keeping things 'shiny and new.' They know how to dig in, work the land and make sacrifices for the small farm towns to thrive. They are not given to nursing their wounds. They get on with it. They give 100 % and then discuss how they can better reach their communities. With so few people and resources, this place demands everything they have. Yet they never complain.

But like the world over, there are also many hearts, dry and cracking, **buried under duty and sacrifice with the** *'Shoulds'* ready to pounce. Religion makes us swallow a strange concoction of *'to whom much is given, much is expected'* and *'noblesse oblige'* to win souls for Jesus, praying that we might not disappoint our Heavenly Father.

It is a life of goodness with a sting in its tail.

And the enemy of my soul pursues me like Javert does Jean Valjean in Les Miserables, threatening that I am nothing more than the sum of my failures, 24601, whispering that this fatigue-filled life of duty and law is the WAY, the TRUTH and the LIFE.[94]

And quite suddenly, I know I am afraid. I fear and doubt myself— maybe Christianity really is about falling into line dutifully.

"Martha, Martha, you are worried and upset about many things, but only one thing is needed. Mary has chosen what is better…and it will not be taken away from her."[95]

94 Crowe, Russell and Jackman, Hugh. *Les Misérables*. DVD. Directed by Tom Hooper. New York City: Universal Pictures, 2012
95 Luke 10:41-42

Mary knew Jesus wanted her, not just the meal she could cook. She sat at the feet of Jesus. She chose intimacy over duty. And as I ponder this, *Grace* surprises me with a kiss and sings over me: *"Your worth isn't in what you do but in who you are to Me!"*

"If anyone is thirsty, let him come to me and drink. Whoever believes in me, as the Scripture has said, streams of living water will flow from within him."[96]

First intimacy, then ministry. All life flows out from the source.

Why is that so hard to do?

Is it arrogance, shame or autonomy that makes me think I need to do something for God?

Is it fear of what others might think? Martha got mad at Mary for 'sitting down.'

Maybe I don't know how to have a relationship with God…or maybe I am secretly terrified of being known by the Almighty?

All the above?

None of the above?

Then there is, of course, the matter of trust. Who doesn't have hidden wounded places in the deep recesses of their hearts, where bits and pieces of enemy shrapnel have lodged and slowly infected their souls with fear, rage, envy and doubt?

A friend once saw a picture when she was praying for herself. She saw herself like a bride on her wedding night. She was in a robe tied up to her neck, hiding in a closet, afraid of her groom and the intimacy she had not yet encountered. The Lord was the groom. And He was seeking her, pursuing her, not daunted by her fear, but certain, as the Lover of her soul, how to woo her.

"Place me like a seal over your heart, like a seal on your arm; for love is as strong as death, its jealousy unyielding as the grave. It burns like blazing fire, like a mighty flame. Many waters cannot quench love; rivers cannot wash it away…"[97]

---

96 John 7:37b-38
97 Song of Solomon 8:6-7

Jesus isn't a salesman at my door hoping I will buy into His program. Rather, He is a suitor, with a red rose in his hand, asking me to marry Him. He calls me Beloved.

Maybe it's easier to just do church and call it good.

"I know your deeds, your hard work and your perseverance. I know that you cannot tolerate wicked men, that you have tested those who claim to be apostles but are not and have found them false. You have persevered and have endured hardships for my name and have not grown weary. Yet, I hold this against you: You have forsaken your first love."[98]

There is only one great commandment given.

"Love the Lord your God with all your heart

...and with all your soul

...and with all your strength

... and with all your mind.

And Love your neighbour as yourself."[99]

A girlfriend had read it in the scriptures: *"Love must be sincere."[100]*

She said it as a joke, but it never left the air. "Sincerely? I thought I was doing a good job, just trying to fake it!"

***

I glance up. The rain has stopped.

A short shower for the earth, that's it? Is this *living water* promise real? Is God teasing us?

Several of my newfound friends recently gathered around my kitchen table. Munching on fresh baked bread and muffins, we began to discover through a meandering conversation that we had all lost a baby

---

98   Revelation 2:2-4
99   Matthew 22:37b
100 Romans 12:9

91

of our own. Slowly, one by one, each woman risked remembering and sharing about the baby she had carried, two of the women to full term, only for the infant to die. Just an informal Bible study group, but there the Lord was patiently weaving together hearts that had survived and moved on, but were somewhere in the deep, afraid to trust, believe, hope.

Words just shared with me yesterday by a frustrated gentleman ring through my ears: "As far as I am concerned, all that gets birthed around here is disillusionment and despair." And I can't help but think of my friends, feeling life growing, burgeoning within them, only to come to the great day of anticipation and instead of meeting life, death arrives instead.

Is there a redeemer able to save? Can anything or anyone revive hope to the disillusioned and bring joy for despair?

Maybe it's sinful to even ask—sacrilegious?

It has been said to despair is to turn your back on God.

But then there it is written down in the black and white of the Holy Book, the ancient words of the prophet Jeremiah's own struggle: ***"Why is my pain unending and my wound grievous and incurable? Will you be to me like a deceptive brook, like a spring that fails?"[101]***

Does God toy with us? Is the little bit of rain the carrot dangled before us?

If He *can*, why doesn't He?

Everything churns within me; my soul feels the burn at the back of the throat. I can feel the torrent of questions ready to spew evidence of the decay and waste that has formed in the bogs of my own heart.

If He can heal all our diseases, why did I watch my father waste away?

If He is the author of life, why were the arms of those mamas left achingly empty as another grave filled?

If His arm is righteous to save, why did He not protect the little Muslim girl shown on the news who had acid poured all over her face by vile men?

---

101 Jeremiah 15:18

At best, are you asleep, God? At worst, are you playing some sadistic game with us?

"Let this Christ, this King of Israel, come down now from the cross, that we may see and believe. "He saved others," they said, "but he can't save himself."[102]

Hmmm…apparently, I am not the first to ask, nor the first to want to see God act.

The religious leaders and the criminal wanted to see Him prove His power and mighty acts.

He didn't.

Jesus didn't save himself, pull himself down off the cross.

He didn't prove Himself to the critics taunting him.

"He will not let your foot slip –he who watches over you will not slumber; indeed, he who watches over Israel will neither slumber nor sleep. The Lord watches over you—the Lord is your shade at your right hand; the sun will not harm you by day, nor the moon by night." [103]

Is this true God? Because your seeming absence in certain situations makes it seem as if perhaps you do sleep?

The commentary interprets the Psalm further: *He not only protects those whom he is the keeper of, but he refreshes them: He is their shade. The comparison has a great deal of gracious condescension in it; the eternal Being who is infinite substance is what he is in order that he may speak sensible comfort to his people, promises to be their umbra —their shadow, to keep as close to them as the shadow does to the body and to shelter them from the scorching heat, as the shadow of a great rock in a weary land.*[104]

It is a beautiful theological explanation.

But my heart doesn't accept theological explanations as such.

---

102 Mark 15:31-32
103 Psalm 121:3-4
104 Blueletterbible.org, "Psalm 121:3-4," accessed October 14, 2019, https://www.blueletterbible.org/Comm/mhc/Psa/Psa_121.cfm

Instead it convulses violently remembering its own anguish seventeen years before and searches for an answer. It is my heart that stores the smell of antiseptic, records the sterile semi-private room and the longing for my out-of-town-husband. It reacts to the deep feelings of shame as the buckets filled with blood and something good turning terribly wrong as I re-hear the echo of my own voice calling out, *"I just want to see the baby."* My heart writhes afresh in pain, remembering the doctor's stoic manner as he dealt with the placenta and ordered the drugs and DNC. And then my own memory seems dimmed but for one thing…

My father came. He left his work and came to the hospital.

He was there and as all turned blurry, I remember only this, his tears falling on my face.

My daddy, weeping for his daughter's pain and anguish, holding me as my world collapsed.

He became my shade in the inferno of that hellish day.

My heart responds to this. Fear, shame, pain, all melt in the memory of my father's love.

And then I hear it, a still small voice, a heavenly whisper…

"That is why I stayed on the cross. Let me be your shade now, Sarah. Let me be as close as your shadow is to your body."

I can feel theology trying to move beyond my intellect into my emotions, into deep understanding.

Is it true that if Jesus had proven Himself—saved himself, there would not be any healing for the decayed places in my soul?

Is it true that love compelled him to stay, endure the cross, the jeers, so that my soul would know that I am not alone?

God is love.

Emmanuel: God with us.

I can feel the Spirit trying to break through a thick, callous religious space within me.

"Truth is a person...not a belief. And Truth is not sadistic, negligent or impotent."

Jesus, like my father, cries with me, promising to absorb all my pain, despair and antagonism into his passion, his death and resurrection, in order that I might have hope and life.

"My God, my God, why hast thou forsaken me? That was a cry of utter God-forsakenness, the despairing cry of man in his dereliction which Jesus had made his own...But there in the depths where we are exposed to the final judgments of God, Jesus converted man's atheistical shout of abandonment and desolation into a prayer of commitment and trust, "Father unto thy hands I commend my spirit."[105]

My doubt, my weariness, my lack of understanding, my antagonism towards God, my despair—this is why Jesus died. Jesus descended *"into the very hell of our godlessness and despair, laying fast hold of us and taking our cursed condition upon himself, in order to embrace us forever in his reconciling love."[106]*

Lenses are being adjusted. Is it not the very passion of Christ that demands more from us? Is it not His love holding us, engulfing us that reveals our own reluctance and natural bent to prefer anything but Him? Maybe it is actually more comfortable to live with a sigh in our voice, asking, '*Are you really out there, God?*' than to be consumed by divine truth and steady love. This all-pervading love knows how to bring light to the darkest recesses of our soul, reaching for even the unknown poisonous doubts and fears.

Am I willing?

Maybe the bride doesn't fear the groom as much as being made vulnerable; am I afraid of being exposed?

Fierce Love pierces my darkness. The Lover of my soul will not reject my bared soul. Present doubts of God's goodness vanish, fears of the old order returning are laid down for this moment.

Truth declares afresh: I AM is Love.

---

105 Thomas Torrance, *The Mediation of Christ*, (Colorado Springs, Helmers & Howard, 1992), 43
106 Torrance, *The Mediation of Christ*, 43

Once again, Grace like rain is falling. Drink my soul, drink!

"Come thou fount of every blessing, tune my heart to sing thy grace. Streams of mercy, never ceasing, call for songs of loudest praise. Teach me some melodious sonnet sung by flaming tongues above. Praise His name, I'm fixed upon it. Name of God's redeeming love."[107]

---

107 Robert Robinson, *Come Thou Fount of Every Blessing*, 1757

baptism

an invitation to dance with the lover of our souls

"Faith is the bird that feels the light and sings when the dawn is still dark."

-Rabindranath Tagore

As my thirst becomes satisfied, this stream of grace pumping life into every cell of my body, my hunger pains become more recognizable. More specific questions rumble their longing for an answer in the abdomen of my soul.

My spirit grabs hold of *I AM's* love, while my soul tries to catch up. My soul still has questions, doubts.

"Blessed are you who hunger now, for you will be satisfied."[108]

Really, God?

"Her breathing is shallower today."

That's what the email from the church member said and a familiar lump fills my throat as it remembers that kind of sound as my father lay dying.

It's sleeting outside. The temperature has dropped.

The definition in the dictionary is clinical:

Leukaemia: any of several cancers of the bone marrow that prevent the normal manufacture of red and white blood cells and platelets, resulting in anemia, increased susceptibility to infection and impaired blood clotting.[109]

It doesn't make any sense; these things never do. The definition doesn't mention anything about emotional bombs exploding. It doesn't seem to register the shock of yet another first-time mom going into premature labour four weeks early.

---

108 Luke 6:21
109 Dictionary.com, 'Leukaemia,' accessed Oct 12,2019, https://www.dictionary.com/browse/leukemia?s=t

97

It wasn't supposed to happen this way.

Nor the inexplicable alarm upon seeing the black and blue bruising underneath the milky white vernix of her new-born babe.

Surely, it will be alright?

Nor the devastation when the white coats say, "I am sorry…*there is nothing else we can do*. We don't think your little Georgina Grace will make it past the weekend."

Georgina Grace means farmer of grace.

Really? Only in an upside-down kingdom can grace be found in an F5 tornado.

"I tell you the truth, unless a kernel of wheat falls to the ground and dies, it remains only a single seed."[110]

What can one do?

They *choose* to hold, cherish, savour every moment granted with their long anticipated eight-day old daughter. It is announced in church that on Saturday they went to the Botanical gardens. They dressed the little farmer of grace so prettily, met grandma and grandpa, aunts and uncles for family photos and held a special baptismal service. Water sprinkled on the little angel, dedicating her to her Maker, laying her in the Almighty's care.

Baptism: a trying or purifying experience or initiation.[111]

She is not the only one being baptised. We see her beautiful little face sleeping in her mama's arms up on the screen in church; every father's face solemn, every mother's heart wrenching at the threat of this mama's hopes and dreams being buried as deep as six feet under.

Sniffs and tears permeate the Sanctuary. Worship begins and I am surprised. Surprised at the incredible release to sing out my tears and pain as an offering mixed up with that of my friends. And I am not the only one; something powerful is happening. As we sing to the

---

110 John 12:24
111 Dictionary.com, 'Baptism,' accessed Oct 12, 2019, https://www.dictionary.com/browse/baptism?s=t

Almighty and petition for little Georgina Grace, this little reserved farming community seems to be coming to life; almost a strange little miracle in and of itself. Carefully built walls around hearts are being made vulnerable; intercession is gushing through the normally carefully hidden cracks of our souls. Just eight days old and this little Farmer of Grace's life is already impacting the land around her in some strange upside-down way…

Grace like rain *is* beginning to fall across the room.

***

My mind swirls, "How shall I pray, God?"

The hunger rumbles loudly in my soul. It seems that I was just here, wondering how to pray for my father. Once again, I am in this tension. I believe God can heal, but will he? Some say if we have enough faith, we can persuade God, that He will inhabit our faith and do a miracle.

Jenny Savage, my precious Sunday School teacher taught us that Elijah was a man just like us. As a ten-year-old girl I understood her to mean that he was an ordinary human like us, a hunk of flesh and blood who believed God to do extraordinary things and because he believed, saw God do miracles.

"The prayer of a righteous man is powerful and effective. Elijah was a man just like us. He prayed earnestly that it would not rain, and it did not rain on the land for three and half years. Again, he prayed, and the heavens gave rain, and the earth produced its crops."[112]

I have heard and I have seen God answer prayers in miraculous ways. But I have also seen God not answer prayers in the way that had been hoped. Do prayers depend upon my own righteousness or level of faith? I fear that perhaps my prayers for my father were ineffective because of my lack of righteousness. Had I been a perfect saint…would it have made any difference? Must I behave just right, believe without any doubt for my prayers to count?

Feeling somewhat anxious, I look up the Greek word for Elijah's righteousness. It is *dikaios* and means to be *approved by God* to be *just*

---

112 James 5:16b-18

in the eyes of God.[113]

How do I know that you approve of me, God? What justifies me in your eyes?

"So, we too, have put our faith in Christ Jesus that we may be justified by faith in Christ and not by observing the law, because by observing the law no one will be justified."[114]

I exhale a sigh of relief that my faith, though shaken of late, is in Christ.

"Praise the Lord, O my soul, and forget not all his benefits…who forgives all your sins and heals all your diseases, who redeems your life from the pit and crowns you with love and compassion."[115]

If healing is part of the cross and grace is unconditional and for the asking, why would I have to conjure up enough strength or faith of my own to twist God's arm to heal?

How then shall I stand in this?

I hear a baby girl crying loudly with us in the church sanctuary. Her auntie takes her to the back. *The Presence* prompts me to go and ask the baby's name; I thought perhaps her name might be Hope or Grace, crying for and with us. Instead, her name is Indie. Although I am delighted to meet this Indie, as that is the nickname for my own niece, Indigo Rain, I am disappointed that there isn't some sign or understanding of how to intercede as I had hoped.

I return to my seat and pray a scripture that comes to mind.

"As you lay there in your blood, I said to you, "Live."[116]

O God, we need a blood transfusion. You shed your blood on Calvary. Does your blood work in this situation? Could you give your blood for Georgina's toxic blood? It says by your stripes we are healed. If only you could confound the Doctors as you did with my niece, Indigo Rain…

---

113 Biblehub.com, "Righteous; James 5:16," accessed October 14, 2019, https://biblehub.com/greek/1342.htm
114 Galatians 2:16
115 Psalm 103:2
116 Ezekiel 16:6

BAM! Light bulb on!

A sudden sunbeam streams through the side window in the sanctuary onto my face and I feel God's pleasure at my sudden understanding. The baby's name that I enquired of was Indie! My own Indie, Indigo Rain, was a miracle baby; the doctors had declared my sister barren. The meaning was clear: Go ahead and ask.

"Ask and you shall receive."[117]

Immediately, I am sceptical. What if I ask and I am disappointed? What if I am played the fool?

I see the Lord before me asking, -*"Will you have this dance?"*

"How can I dance if I am trying to take a stand?"

"Take a stand to dance! Choose to dance with me...where I lead."

I am not sure what God is asking of me. Please define.

Dictionary.com obliges: *"to move one's feet or body, or both, rhythmically in a pattern of steps, especially to the accompaniment of music."*

And I ponder what it looks like to step where God steps in this and I wonder what song He has in mind?

The piano on Pandora is playing an almost music-box like tune. I am momentarily swayed by the vision of a pink ballerina twirling in an old jewellery box of mine. But the real choice is before me; I am not being called to a solo dance. Am I willing to take his hand? Step out onto that dance floor and swirl with the Author of life? Am I willing to swing way out wide, barely holding on, *all those questions and doubts* and then allow Him to swing me back into Him, cheek to cheek? It's an invitation to intimacy, to trust.

And then I feel reluctant. Who don't I trust? Myself, Him, maybe both?

Someone once said to me, "Don't dance. You don't have any rhythm." What if I do this wrong? Make a fool out of myself, but even more my partner? It's one thing to face my own limitations, but another thing to mar God's reputation.

---

117 John 16:24

But there He stands, his hand extended, waiting. He can handle His own reputation. And my spirit grasps that it would PLEASE God to *choose* this dance, to pray for, hope for, believe for a miracle and *trust Him* for the outcome.

Asking is a way in which I lift my eyes to Him, trusting, expecting all His goodness.

There it is again to *trust.* I know I don't trust myself. *Do I trust Him?* In theory it doesn't seem like much to step out onto the dance floor and believe that God will lead...

But in reality, to trust, knowing...

>He can GIVE and TAKE AWAY life,

>He IS GOOD (all the time) but NOT TAME,

>And to be OK with the outcome,

>Even. If. It's. Not. The. Way. I. Want. It!

...that is another thing entirely.

Or is it?

Maybe the point of any dance is just that; to STOP trying to control outcomes and *move in a way that is transformed by the music.*

I note the scripture and see a similar dance between Abraham and God. Abraham asked for the city of Sodom to be spared from impending doom. And God said 'Yes' more than once. His nephew, Lot, was delivered out of Sodom, but in the end, Sodom was destroyed by raining sulphur.

WHAT?

Why did God say 'Yes' he would save and then didn't spare the city? Why does he seem pleased to reveal His desire to say 'Yes' to Abraham even when the outcome is different to what was asked for? That does not make me feel confident about asking for little Georgina's life to be spared. More like a fool about to be played *again.*

"And so, when God destroyed the cities of the plain, he remembered Abraham, and he brought Lot out of the catastrophe that overthrew the cities where Lot had lived."[118]

Abraham never asked God to spare Lot's life. Was he afraid that his nephew was not righteous enough? Was he afraid God might object on the grounds of nepotism? If the dance is really about the relationship between the two dancing, what is God revealing of Himself in this intimate dance with Abraham?

"Yes. I AM who you think I am. I am not a bloodthirsty God like the Gods of the heathen nations around you. I am for life. It is not my heart to destroy. And what matters to you, matters to me." –

It's as if *God's 'Yes'* was to the hidden unspoken questions of Abraham's heart.

Do I have hidden unspoken questions in my heart?

Jesus asked those he healed, "What do you want?"

Good question!

***

And there it is written on my email;

"Georgina Grace passed away peacefully in her father's arms last night."

I wonder what kind of dance this is.

Once again, the ladies gather here around the well-worn farmhouse coffee table. My friend who knows the pain of labouring two stillborn babies chokes back tears as she tells us about the private funeral.

They made it a celebration of life. Amid a hovering rainbow of balloons, the father shared every detail he could remember of his precious daughter's nine days of life. An auntie read Hairy Maclary. And then the brave mama stood and sang. She sang over her firstborn lying still in her manger, and like the privileged shepherds of long ago, the people knew that they were on holy ground. Bubbles were blown and floated upwards as the pallbearers exited with the miniature coffin, while an unearthly hope descended upon those left behind.

---

118 Genesis 19:29

The depth of pain and beauty swirling from the words of the event takes all our breath away. This little pink ballerina in her box, Georgina Grace, plays to a heavenly melody and every time it is remembered, the sound of another world will be heard.

My mind turns to see the empty arms of Georgina Grace's parents and all I can think is that their dance is as costly and exquisite as a diamond. Everyone loves to be on the winning side, a victory dance, but to watch someone dance with all their heart, soul and mind among ashes is unforgettable. This dance—this *dance of Job*, leaves an indelible mark upon hearts.

"At this Job got up and tore his robe and shaved his head. Then he fell to the ground in worship and said:

"Naked I came from mother's womb, and naked I will depart. The Lord gave and the Lord has taken away; may the name of the Lord be praised."[119]

A golden wheat field ripples like waves on the sea as it dances with the wind. It yields, surrenders, and flexes— with every breath the air inhales and exhales. I always thought it would be wonderful to be able to dance like that.

What if we are the wheat and God is the wind?

Yahweh.

Jehovah.

I remember that the Hebrew name for God is pronounced like the sounds of breathing.

God is as intimate and near as the very air we breathe.

To watch the stunning *dance of Job* left me momentarily breathless. Is that why God seems so far away in such times?

I read these words this morning:

"What if, in truth, our God is the party planner? (Didn't he say he was preparing a wedding feast for us and building mansions in heaven?) What if the same God who created a breath-taking garden, planned

---

119 Job 1:20-21

purpose and the love of family and friendship and the fulfilment of
productive work, who delighted in children, who touched the sick and
*rejected and who gave grace to the prostitutes and tax collectors **is** the*
God whose companionship we can enjoy each day?"[120]

Did Abraham believe this? Did he suspect that the one true God was less fire and brimstone and more relational? What then must he have thought of his Good God when Sodom was destroyed? And again, when he was challenged to sacrifice his son?

Did he have the breath knocked out of him, too?

Did he feel the quality of air we breathe called into question?

Did he hear the masked voice of Eden's serpent whispering doubts;

"Are you sure God really said???"

"He's holding back on you!"

"He's not really for you! He's not who you think He is! In fact, He doesn't really exist…!"

Is God still God, still good…when the bombs go off in our life?

"He makes his winds messengers, his servants flames of fire?"[121]

What then do we make of the devastation left in the wake of tornadoes and hurricanes?

What is the message?

***

Two messages rang in this week, one from the doctor, one from my sister.

Again, black clouds seem to be gathering…looming…

My stomach tightens with the first call. I am informed that I need to take some more tests; my CA-125 scores are double what they should be.

---

120 Sally Clarkson. *Dancing with My Father: How God Leads Us into a Life of Grace and Joy.* (Colorado Springs: Waterbrook Press, 2010) https://sallyclarkson.com/blog/2019/5/3/holy-joy-dancing-with-my-heavenly-father-chapter-two
121 Psalm 104:4

"It doesn't necessarily mean you have ovarian cancer—but...."

The second call comes from my sister in the emergency room of an American hospital. She has been given antibiotics for a severe breast infection, but more tests are needed to rule out the kind of lump that every woman fears to find.

The threats hang heavy. Not even having been very long since we laid our father to rest, the ravenous cancer beast seems hellbent on sinking its teeth into new blood.

I fight my thoughts. Try to defend myself from the "what if" arrows shooting hard and fast.

Too late!

What if I do have cancer?

What if I must do chemo? Can I lose my hair graciously? Seriously— how can I worry about my hair at such a time as this?

How will I support my husband with his work—he can't manage the kids too?

And the kids, who will be able to help them through their days? What if it's advanced? To not be able to see them grow old, get married, have children?

Indeed, what if the tumour is not benign? What if it is not only malignant...but terminal? What if this is the end—right now, in what is supposed to be the very middle of my life?

I see my children's faces again...and I can't even think...

My eldest overhears the call. She storms into my room with her arms crossed tight against her chest and defiantly declares, "If God lets you or Auntie die, I will never speak to Him again!"

Do you know what you are doing, God?

It is even harder not to worry for my sis. As the older one, it's always been my job to look after her. In my mind's eye, I see the squeals of delight when my niece sees her mama, how the tot seems to literally draw strength from my sister as she pulls herself up on her mama's legs. Surely God, you would not leave this long-awaited gift, this promised child, Indigo Rain, without a mommy to nurture her?

He gives and takes away...

My worries gain momentum as I recall that both my sis and I had dreams one week apart a year ago that we were in a black time, but that things were about to get blacker. Mine ended with me losing all my hair. Hers ended with black crows descending, a symbol of death. The threats of losing hair to chemo or a sister to breast cancer after such a couple of hard years seems unbearable.

God wouldn't allow that, would he?

But didn't he allow that mama to lose her little *farmer of grace*?

The hunger burns...*who is this God?*

theory
an invitation to be refined

"You need chaos in your soul to give birth to a dancing star."

-Friedrich Nietzsche

Who is this God?

The question gnaws in my soul gut, revealing the empty and painful places that were once satisfied. What I did know, now feels empty. All the calories that I have consumed in my life have been used up in this adventure. I am in desperate need of something solid to sink my teeth into… I am starving.

"Blessed are those who are hungry now, for they shall be satisfied."[122]

Suddenly I am hearing a voice ask me a twenty-year-ago question, now, again.

Her name was Muriel. She was beautiful, erect and refined. White hair framed her face, a crown of wisdom upon her head. I was a novice counsellor to teenage girls and a newly pregnant mama with my eldest daughter. I was growing heavy, weary with the caseload I was under and in her experience, she took me to the word of God.

But first she told me a story, followed by a question. If questions could smack, I would have been knocked to the ground.

Friends of hers were missionaries in South America. They had given up everything to follow the call of God. They raised their beautiful daughter away from family and the comforts of the American dream. They were proud parents on the night of her graduation. After the celebration they stayed back to clean up as their daughter, boyfriend and two other couples went for a midnight stroll on the beach.

Their daughter never came back.

Thugs jumped the group, raped and killed the girls in front of their boyfriends and left the boys for half dead.

---

122 Luke 6:21

Then Muriel asked me the question, a question relevant for the now…

"When someone comes to you in such devastation and asks *where is God in all of this*…how will you answer?

I choked on air, my own spit, fighting to breathe.

How should I know? Where was God? How could he let those things happen especially to such good people, people who had given their lives to him?

Is this God the same God who saved Noah by having him build an ark, closed the mouth of lions while Daniel was in the den, or answered Elijah's prayers with fire from heaven? Is this the same God who helped David slay Goliath, had caused the walls of Jericho to fall with one mighty shout and transformed Joseph's years of hardship into a diploma for leadership?

Hebrews says that all these things came about because of faith. Do we not have enough faith these days? Or could something more be going on?

Muriel put the Good Book in my hands and had me turn the pages to Job chapter one.

I read about a God-fearing, righteous man named Job, who was known as the greatest man in the East. Not only was he a good man, but he was wealthy and had ten children, a sign of God's blessing and favour. The only weakness exposed in Job was his fear that his children might not revere God so he offers sacrifices each morning on their behalf.

Was he afraid that God might smite them? Or even him?

If so, all his worst nightmares come true. Within minutes all his oxen, donkeys and camels are stolen, his sheep are burned up by fire falling from heaven, his servants murdered and children found dead underneath the rubble of a house struck by a mighty wind.

Processing the thought of such devastation in my own life, I submit to the leading of my own silver haired sage.

"First," she said, "Re-read the chapter. Does God cause these things?"

I note the bizarre exchange in heaven.

Satan comes before the Lord and answers the Lord's question, "Where have you come from?" semi-truthfully. *From roaming through the earth and going back and forth in it.*[123]

The devil's response conveniently omits 'why': "...*Your enemy the devil prowls around like a roaring lion, looking for someone to devour.*"[124]

God knew what Satan could do. Yet the proud papa in him says, *"Have you considered my servant Job? There is no one on earth like him; he is blameless and upright, a man who fears God and shuns evil."*[125]

Again, Satan answers with a partial truth.

"Does Job fear God for nothing? Have you not put a hedge around him and his household and everything he has? You have blessed the work of his hands, so that his flocks and herds are spread through the land. But stretch out your hand and strike everything he has, and he will surely curse you to your face."[126]

Satan knows that God would not strike Job.

God then grants Satan permission to mess with Job, but not to lay a hand on Job himself.

The result: Job suffers heavy losses.

It is not enough. Satan returns another day from roaming all over the earth and once again stands before the Lord with all the angels.

God points out Job's integrity and faithfulness even when Satan tried to incite him to ruin without any reason.

Satan ups the stakes.

"Skin for skin! Satan replied. "A man will give all he has for his own life. But stretch out your hand and strike his flesh and bones, and he will surely curse you to your face."

123 Job 1:6-7
124 1 Peter 5:8
125 Job 1:8
126 Job 1:9-11

The Lord said to Satan, "Very well, then, he is in your hands; but you must spare his life."[127]

Satan then inflicts Job with heavy sores from head to toe.

What is going on???

***

Muriel has me read Colossians 3:3.

"*...Your life...*" She holds up her pointing finger to represent my life.

"*...is now hidden in Christ...*" She wraps her other hand around her pointer finger.

"*...in God.*"[128] She removes her finger and wraps that hand around the outside of the other one.

"Do you see?" she asks. "When we believe in Jesus, we have a double hedge of protection about us. Nothing can affect us unless we ourselves choose to step outside of the hedge, or God allows something in."

I ponder before I articulate, "So what you are saying is that God did not cause Job's pain, but he did allow it."

"Yes," she responded. "God does not cause evil. Evil comes from the lion seeking to devour. But when evil comes up against one of his righteous, God has allowed it."

She gently presses, "Why do you think He would do that?"

Bible still in my hands she asks me to turn the pages to Luke 22:31: *"Simon, Simon, Satan has asked to sift you as wheat. But I have prayed for you, Simon, that your faith may not fail. And when you have turned back, strengthen your brethren."*

Silently I am thinking, "Really, we go through hell and back to identify with someone else's pain? Is that really fair, necessary?"

Muriel interrupts my thoughts with a question: "Sarah, what happens when things are sifted? When you sift flour for a cake?"

---

127 Job 2:4-6
128 Colossians 3:3

"They are refined. The bad stuff is separated from the good stuff."

"Yes," she answered. "What would happen if we just sifted flour in the wind?"

"It would all blow away into nothing."

"Yes," she said again. "But if I put a big bowl under it?"

"It would catch all the refined flour, made smooth and perfect for the main ingredient in something like a cake."

She then asked: "Why then do you think God might allow us to be sifted?"

I gave the obvious answer, "To refine us."

Refine: to bring to a fine or a pure state; free from impurities[129]

Do I see sifting, all the pain, as a process for freedom from myself, that I may become more like Him?

"Consider it a sheer gift, friends, when tests and challenges come at you from all sides. You know that under pressure, your faith-life is forced into the open and shows its true colours. So, don't try to get out of anything prematurely. Let it do its work, so you become mature and well-developed, not deficient in any way."[130]

"Where is God in the sifting process?" she asked.

I looked at the verse again. "Praying…."

Jesus is praying for me when I don't know where He is, when I can't feel His presence, that my faith will not fail. Jesus is interceding for me when I don't know how to pray.

Coming out of my long-ago memory, I proceed to think of how I felt when I read the words that Georgina had passed away.

I said to the Lord, "SEE! I KNEW IT! It's too risky to consider dancing with you. I prayed a scripture in faith for Georgina, *"as you lay there in your blood, I said to you live."* Well, where has that gotten us? -The whole thing is a bloody mess!

---

129 Dictionary.com, 'Refine,' accessed October 12, 2019, https://www.dictionary.com/browse/refine?s=t
130 James 1:1 (MSG)

"And when I had passed by you and saw you wallowing in your blood, I said to you in your blood, 'Live!' I said to you in your blood, 'Live!'"[131]

An unexpected voice now says to me, *"As you lay there in your blood Sarah, I say to you live."*

"In the same way, the Spirit helps us in our weakness. We do not know what we ought to pray for, but the Spirit himself intercedes for us with groans that words cannot express."[132]

***

Just a few months down the road from my talk with silver sage Muriel, I held my own first born. At just eight weeks, I laid her growing chubby body gently on the crackly paper covering the doctors table to get her first set of shots. She looked up at me and gave me a real genuine smile (not one of those gassy ones). She looked me in the eyes and seemed to know that I was for her and smiled. Just as she did, the nurse gave her 4 shots. Eyes still on me, her smile turned into shock. She looked at me as if I had betrayed her and the screams began.

I cried. I cried even after I had scooped her up and comforted her, redressed her and put her in her car seat. All the way home, I cried.

She didn't know that I was not the one to administer the shots. She just knew that she looked to me with trust… and pain had come upon her suddenly. She didn't know that I had allowed the nurse to inflict her with the pain in hopes of fortifying her system and preventing her premature death.

She didn't know that I had allowed this pain for her good, so that she could grow up healthy and strong.

And then I heard the Lord. *"Now you know just a little bit more of my heart."*

His heart is for us. His plans are for our good, our best, and he cries for and with us, interceding on our behalf when the shots of life jab into us.

Did Job know this in the deep? Had he walked closely enough with God to suspect, like Abraham, that God was deeply for him, despite

---

131 Ezekiel 16:6
132 Romans 8:26

113

that the world around him would have believed that the gods were beings to appease?

For Job's response is stunning: *"At this (all the bad news), Job got up and tore his robe and shaved his head. Then he fell to the ground in worship."*[133]

Worship???

Obviously not an upbeat praise and dance time. Job was not in denial, refusing to grieve. In his grief, he somehow worships.

In fact, Job's wife says to him, *"Are you still holding on to your integrity? Curse God and die!"*[134]

Job responds, *"You are talking like a foolish woman. Shall we accept good from God, and not trouble?"*[135]

Wasn't that Satan's goal in the Garden of Eden, to get Adam and Eve to doubt God's goodness—to get them to curse God and die?

I recall Muriel having me turn pages to Psalm 50.

I read:

"Do I eat the flesh of bulls or drink the blood of goats? Sacrifice thank offerings to God, fulfil your vows to the Most High, and call upon me in the day of trouble; I will deliver you, and you will honour me. ... He who sacrifices thank offerings honours me, and he prepares the way so that I may show him the salvation of God."[136]

Was that what it was that Job offered as worship—a sacrifice of thanksgiving?

Sacrifice: *the offering of animal, plant, or human life or of some material possession to a deity, as in propitiation or homage.*[137]

Homage: *respect or reverence paid or rendered*[138]

---

133 Job 1:20
134 Job 2:9
135 Job 2:10
136 Psalm 15:13-15, 23
137 Dictionary.com, 'Sacrifice,' accessed October 12, 2019, https://www.dictionary.com/browse/sacrifice?s=t
138 Dictionary.com, 'Homage,' accessed October 12, 2019, https://www.dictionary.com/browse/homage?s=t

Propitiate: *to make favorably inclined; appease; conciliate.*[139]

The surrounding nations would have tried to make propitiation to their gods. They would have tried to appease their various gods with fertility rituals, dancing and offering up livestock, human lives and newborn babies.

But this God of Job, the God of the Hebrews, is not interested in such worship. He doesn't want more rituals, more blood. He doesn't want to be appeased. He wants to be loved, known and trusted.

Job's sacrifice of thanksgiving does just that. Job cries, tears his robe, falls to the ground and trusts. He sacrifices his thanks when none seems to be in order because he believes somewhere in the deep that God is good and will make good to him.

"I don't understand what's happening, God. But I know you and you are good. You love me and I can trust that you will bring something of infinite value from the circumstances I now walk in."

And God seems blessed, loved by Job's offering.

Is that the point of this dance? Is it an opportunity to love and bless God not just for the obvious good things He regularly gives us, things we often feel entitled to, but to declare who He is to us even when things are not going grand, based on who He declares himself to be?

My mind flashes to the days of being a young bride. I remember our first fight—the passionate seemingly righteous indignation that we both felt. I threatened the word *divorce*. In my own heart and mind, I was not yet fully committed, even sure of my decision.

My husband reeled backwards. And then with what strength he had he gently took me by my shoulders, looked me in the eyes and said, "We made a commitment before God and each other. Divorce is not an option. We will work this out."

I knew he was right. But even more, I understood in the depths of my heart that he was committed to us, to our good.

---

139 Dictionary.com, 'Propitiate,' accessed October 12, 2019, https://www.dictionary.com/browse/propitiate?s=t

God is committed to me, to my good. Am I willing to say back to Him, "In sickness and in health, even unto death?"

Do I have a theology that crumbles when God doesn't perform the way I think He should? Do I see Him as one to be appeased, served? Do I get angry when I give him all my best and He doesn't perform the way I think He should?

Or do I know Him well enough that, despite what the enemy tries to throw at us (sickness, calamity, even death), I can trust that nothing will part us. His heart is true to me. Is my own heart steadfast?

This dance, the Dance of Job, not only refines and frees us, it rearranges who we are. It invites us into a deeper and more intimate relationship with God. And just like the beauty of seeing a couple who have made it 59 years together and still love each other, is the sacred beauty of this dance of Job.

The scriptures say that, ***"Perfect love casts out fear."*** [140]

Perhaps it is in the dance that the love is made perfect.

I understand in theory that nothing is ever wasted, that the little grace farmer, Georgina Grace's life, as well as that of my father's, has and will continue to serve their purpose.

So, my answer is "Yes." I accept this dance and trust that somehow in it you, God, will answer the unidentifiable questions still lurking in my deep.

In my moment of surrender, I receive a text from my sister.

My sister has been cleared. She is going to see her miracle baby grow up.

I let go a sigh of relief when my phone rings again. It's my doctor:

"The CT scan shows nothing! I don't know how to explain it, but what was there is gone! It's actually a miracle."

Game on, God: Let's dance!

---

140 1 John 4:18

epiphany

an invitation to move beyond dualism

"Miracles begin understated. They begin, and the earth doesn't shake, and trumpets don't sound. Miracles begin with the plain song of a promise—and sometimes not even fully believed. This is always the best place for miracles. God meets us right where we don't believe. When our believing runs out, God's loving runs on."

-Ann Voskamp

I understand that when someone has been extremely thirsty or hungry, water and food must be given in small incremental amounts so that the person can absorb the liquid or substance without getting sick.

Slowly, I am being revived with a little understanding here, a little understanding there. And as keen as I am to accept this dance, there is still something nagging within me. Though the rumbles are lessening, I can still feel a deeply empty place.

I have been weighing it ever since I wrote it: *"It's as if God's 'yes' was to the hidden unspoken questions of Abraham's heart. What are mine? What are yours? Jesus asked those he healed, "What do you want?"*

What are my hidden, unspoken questions?

What do I want?

I search within and can't find just one pointed, clarifying question, today on the anniversary of my father's death. My soul seems to be a cauldron full of simmering odds and ends—questions stewing under the watchful eye of the Almighty chef.

I have heard it said that we learn even more by asking questions than learning the answers. Why then, does it feel like I am in the wrong for asking? Am I weak or just plain stupid for not 'getting it'?

I don't want to be calling God to the stand. Nor do I want to ask questions to accuse. I am not the Queen of Sheba and God is not Solomon, but would you, God, like Solomon, permit me to question you the way the Queen of Sheba did Solomon?

"She came to Solomon and talked about all the things that she cared about, emptying her heart to him. Solomon answered everything she put to him—nothing stumped him. When the Queen of Sheba experienced for herself Solomon's wisdom and saw with her own eyes the palace he had built...it took her breath away."[141]

I pause, wondering if I am walking on the ground of heresy. Instead, the Lover of my Soul, gently speaks reassurance, ever drawing me out. All for love...it's always all for love.

The bits and pieces begin to come forth with a torrent of questions, doubts and strange hope all mixed in together.

You said God, *'Ask and you shall receive,'[142]* I want to know if that's really true?

Are you who I hope you are? Is Jesus of Nazareth as relevant for now as then?

Does it make any difference to pray, to ask for a miracle, to have faith?

"Faith is being certain of what we hope for, and sure of what we do not see."[143]

I had hoped my father would live. I hoped Georgina Grace would live. I had hoped to see you do a miracle.

But they are dead.

"How O God, like Abraham, do you plan to remember us?"

***

I search for clues through old evidence in last year's journal and stumble upon a glued-in scrap of paper: a record of an email between my husband and a co-worker about my father's condition.

"A man came to pray for Sarah's father as she had seen in a vision. As he prayed for Ronn's healing, there was an authority to it because of where he had walked himself in the disease (he himself has been healed from cancer). Ronn had a great night's sleep; he was very alert in the morning and responsive. Now, is he healed? I don't know at this

141 1 Kings 10:2-3 (MSG)
142 John 16:24
143 Hebrews 11:1

stage, but I do know that something seemed to 'break-through'. He is still eating, but still sleeping for large chunks of the day and still on the morphine to manage pain. <u>Our greatest on-going request is that the pain would subside so that we could reduce the heavy narcotics.</u> It would be <u>a massive miracle</u> if God granted these requests."

My father did improve after the healing prayer. Within seven days, he went off every ounce of morphine, his appetite returned and his hair colour began to darken. He was in his right mind and could enjoy his children and grandchildren…right up to the end. He ate steak and strawberry pie for dinner the night he died.

Suddenly, I am struck with an epiphany.   –

For the first time *I can see* in all the written down words… *the dance.*

When my father died, I thought God had just been playing with me, toying with me; it felt like God had been leading me on. *But now, I realise that he has indeed been leading me on, not to mess with me, but to dance!*

I didn't know why I had been led to pray for Dad's healing, or why I had had a fulfilled vision of a stranger coming to pray for Dad. The Preacher Man did start to improve and things felt hopeful. In the end, however, it felt like, "Psych. God doesn't really care. He's going to die anyhow."

But now I see the truth, like Abraham, I was invited to dance.

The theory is becoming experience. The truth is staggering; *God loves it* when we ask for a miracle. His heart is always to say 'YES' to his beloved.

As a young mom, I asked a seasoned set of parents with wonderful children to tell me if there were any mottos or principles that they had lived by. Their response was, *"Never say no, when you can say yes."* God's heart is just like this! Even when justice demanded circumstances to be different from what Abraham had hoped, God still said yes to Abraham's heart in a way that He could.

Grief blinds. All my hope seemed to be buried with my father at sea. But now, dawn is lighting upon my soul. And with it, the darkness of confusion gives way to the rising of the Son and the promise of *Hope beyond hope.*

A still small voice whispers: *"Can you see me? That's what you were hungry for, wanting to see me. To know that 'I Am who I Am' and that I am good. I answered and gave you every miracle I could, even when I knew it was your father's time to come home to me."*

I am dumbfounded.

I have been just like one of the fools on the road to Emmaus. I have been dejected, sad and all this time unable to recognize Jesus right here leading me in the dance.

They said to Jesus about himself, ***"We hoped He was going to be the one to save Israel."***[144] The Jews were so busy looking for a miracle to relieve their burden under Roman oppression, that they could not conceive the height, depth, length and width of God's greater plan of love.

Is that not true for today?

In our desperation, in our thrashing about in pain, we can miss God passing by.

Like Moses, do we not ask, ***"Now show me your glory!"***[145]

And God says 'yes' in a way that will not destroy us.

We then find ourselves, like Moses, between a rock and a hard place. Do we perceive God's hand covering us? And his proclamation over us: ***"I will cause all of my goodness to pass in front of you, and I will proclaim my name, the Lord, in your presence."***[146]

He passes by while we are left wondering about this too-close-for-comfort, hidden, dark spot God has placed us in; *until* He removes His hand. Then we see the fuller proclamation of God's name in the earth, in our lives, His name which means and implies goodness, mercy and compassion.

* * *

It is interesting that God never answers Job's questions. Instead He asks Job a torrent of questions. And although Job cannot answer these questions, the questions reveal God's heart and reality to Job.

---

144 Luke 24:21
145 Exodus 33:18
146 Exodus 33:19

"I admit, I once lived by rumours of you; now I have it all first-hand –from my own eyes and ears! I'm sorry –forgive me. I'll never do that again, I promise! I'll never again live on crusts of hearsay, crumbs of rumour."[147]

Thomas F. Torrance, a chaplain during World War 2, held a dying man in his arms. The dying man looked up into Torrance's face and weakly asked, "Is Jesus really like God?" Two years later, Thomas Torrance sat by a dying elderly Presbyterian parishioner. She implored him also, "Is Jesus really like God?"

Torrance went on to uncover the dualism that many of us approach God with. Jesus loves us, accepts us. But many of us fear that behind his smiling face is someone else. One who is ready to scold and punish us in deep anger.

Maybe that is the one, pointed, clarifying question that has been growing within my soul?

Jesus, are you really the face of God?

How many teachings have I listened to in my life? How many second-hand accounts have I believed?

But when God invites us to dance, it is a first-hand experience.

Like Job, there are many questions that have been raised in my heart that I don't have answers to. But somehow, I am satisfied that God is talking back. I can sink my teeth into the fact that He is leading me in a dance and showing me that He can be trusted.

Once again, I hear, *'Yes! I and the Father are one. And we are love."*

Like a chunk of crusty French bread, I chew on this, not wanting to lose one ounce of its goodness. Its nourishment lends this soul strength, making me ready to travel the next leg of the journey.

---

147 Job 42:5-6 (MSG)

weep.ing

1. expressing grief, sorrow, or any overwhelming emotion by shedding tears
2. tearful
3. tending or liable to cry; given to crying.
4. dripping or oozing liquid.

*"God blesses you who weep now,
for in due time you will laugh."*

Luke 6:21

AFTERMATH YEAR THREE:
CAN GOD PENETRATE MY DEPRESSION?

wasteland

an invitation to let God make my present ugly beautiful

"It's the brilliant who don't deny the dark but who always seek the light in everything. So yeah, go ahead and be astonished. Be astonished by the depths of grief which are but the fountains of the heights of joy; and grief and joy are the same landscape of any soul really alive."

-Ann Voskamp

We stand as she appears on the arm of her father.

Gasps of awe are heard all around me as the ordinarily unpretentious, doe-like virgin stuns us all in her white, strapless, beaded gown. Serene and confident she steadily makes her way down the aisle, eyes on her love.

The groom struggles to stay composed. To propose to her, he must have known he loved her. But in this moment, he seems to be seeing the beauty of his treasure for the first time.

Her father, a minister, escorts her down the aisle and then goes on up ahead of her, turns around to face the couple and begins the ceremony. He pontificates about the purpose of marriage, desperately trying to create distance between himself and the present task of not only performing a wedding ceremony, but also having to let go of his little girl. A tender-hearted man, the façade does not last long and a sudden, unplanned cry into the microphone alerts us all to the personal difficulty of the task at hand.

I swore I'd never cry at weddings.

But the tears run from the corner of my eyes, momentarily making me grateful for whoever invented waterproof mascara.

The beauty of the moment mixes with memories of my own...

On a sweltering hot day in June of 1993, I remember the strength of the man I called *Daddy* steadily leading me towards my own love before switching into preacher mode to perform our ceremony.

123

I don't recall much of his sermon that day. But what is etched into the heart of the girl is his voice cracking when he quoted Tevye from Fiddler on the Roof, *"Is this the little girl I carried?"*[148] And somehow in the deepest place of my soul, I knew that my father loved me, valued me so much that not even his carefully practised composure and polished speech could keep it from me.

I knew it was hard for him that day. But I didn't understand what personal strength it would take for him to release me publicly until I stood before a large crowd to give his eulogy. *"Are these the ashes of the man who has carried me all these years?"*

I turn back to the bride before me, so much beauty and love surrounding her, so much joy. Does she know that it's all sand, slipping its way through the hourglass? Does she know that to the degree that she feels joy, she will know grief?

I have come to understand that the two, joy and grief, cannot exist without the other here on earth. And clearly, I have been learning that the Lord is close to the broken-hearted.

But somehow, I feel as if I should be able to move on now. The Lord has shown me 'home.' He has patiently answered my questions, fed my hunger. But rather than jumping up and moving out, I feel as if I am in some misty wasteland, inching my way across a murky bog.

Where I thought I would have more energy, I feel flat, numb.

Instinctively, I know that I am no longer in the Hunger territory, so I look to the map for what comes next: Weeping.

Haven't I done plenty of that? I have cried more tears these past two years; tears of sadness, fear, hope, joy, frustration and anger. I had no idea that there were so many kinds of leaking. Is there to be more?

Feeling somewhat worried about more weeping, I remind myself that choosing courage to traverse poverty and hunger have brought blessings:

You're blessed when you've lost it all. God's kingdom is there for the finding.[149]

---

148 Bock, Jerry. Fiddler on the Roof : (from the Broadway Musical "Fiddler on the Roof"). [United States] :RCA Victor, 1964.
149 Luke 6:20 (MSG)

I think of heaven's kind eyes piercing through me, meeting me in my 'upside-down', shattering my ideals and inviting me into the truth of home.

You're blessed when you're ravenously hungry. Then you are ready for the Messianic meal.[150]

I think of the invitation to dance, not with principles or beliefs, but with God himself.

Why then did Jesus bless those who travailed through weeping?

The promise seems to be that grief can and will somehow make way for more joy.

Joy???

Joy? Joy like sunshine?

I feel some pressure to manufacture a more joyful spirit as we head out to church this morning. I know I can practice a cheerful and thankful attitude. But I cannot pretend to feel and see sunshine where there is only fog.

Even so, I manage a standard, quick 'hello' or so I think, to a new lady at the morning service.

"My thoughts are not your thoughts, declares the Lord..."[151]

I didn't know that her heart too had been all stretched out to the size of Texas. And that like me she had been wandering lost within herself.

The natural eyes can't see another person's soul, they can only read the clues; a giggle, a tear, arms-crossed, heavy sighs. She gave none.

How could I know that the everyday formality of this greeting would leave *me* undone, tap right into my own places?

She had just returned from a distant country that had seared her senses with its bright colours, pungent spices and forgotten children and was looking at returning to work for an orphanage there.

I said I'd pray for direction, God's leading in her life. It seemed spiritual, the right thing to say in church.

---

150 Luke 6:21 (MSG)
151 Isaiah 55:8

And then I saw it—a glimpse in my mind's eye.

One sock, not much of a vision.

Just a sock. A picture of a sock that had once fit, but whose elastic had been overstretched and now could not stay up properly.

And I knew God saw what my natural eyes could not see.

"He reveals deep and hidden things; he knows what lies in darkness, and light dwells with him."[152]

Come, Holy Spirit.

I asked, knowing all too well the same feeling, if she could relate her life to the sock that I saw? If her life once fit, once made sense, but now didn't and somehow, she couldn't seem to wear it?

Pools formed in her eyes. And she shared that she had been wandering, trying to find her place these past five years.

She had never adjusted to life after Australia. To life after... *he* died.

We cried, held each other in the seemingly vast wasteland and waited for the Presence that supersedes words to bring Light to the darkness.

I prayed silently for her, hearing the echo of my own heart: *O God, this human heart and soul is stretched beyond form, leaving a massive indent, as if a prehistoric dinosaur has stomped right down in the middle of her life. Is there hope for the future? Is there life beyond the primitive reduction she has experienced upon her heart?*

We wait for revelation and God gives his heart.

We wait for revelation...

Instead, God gives His heart.

I see His hand, *His righteous right hand*, equal to the same size as the massive cavity across the land of her soul, rise.

He does not slap her and say, "Come on! Get on with it!"

He takes it and places it right over the gaping hole—and it fills.

---

152 Daniel 2:22

It fills all the spaces—His presence, almost tangible.

And with it comes the unspoken yet understood promise. The war-torn world of the heart is not beyond the hand of the creator of Eden.

"The desert and the parched land will be glad; the wilderness will rejoice and blossom. Like the crocus, it will burst into bloom; it will rejoice greatly and shout for joy."[153]

His presence absorbed strengthens our weary wandering hearts. Hope surges.

"Be strong, do not fear, your God will come."[154]

It is not insignificant, this business of God giving us His heart with His hand covering us.

And I wonder if this is the real sunshine I seek?

"Then will the eyes of the blind be opened and the ears of the deaf unstopped. Then will the lame leap like a deer, and the mute tongue shout for joy. Water will gush forth in the wilderness and streams in the desert."[155]

At the least, I understand that things won't always be like this, feel like this.

My connection with the woman at church was beautiful. What if I had no idea what she was feeling? What if everything had stayed perfect in my life? Would we have connected and felt God's heart together in such a way?

"He has made everything beautiful in its time. He has also set eternity in the human heart, yet no one can fathom what God has done from beginning to end."[156]

If it's true that God makes everything beautiful in its time, can God make my present ugly beautiful? Is this verse to be my North star, my hope, to steer by in what has seemed a trackless wasteland?

---

153 Isaiah 35:1
154 Isaiah 35:4
155 Isaiah 35:5
156 Ecclesiastes 3:11

Yes. I hear it this time with a slight twist: *"He makes all things beautiful in His time."*

And I find myself humming a faint tune of an old hymn:

> *Be still my soul, The Lord is on thy side.*
> *Bear patiently thy cross of grief or pain.*
> *Leave to thy God to order and provide;*
> *In every change, He faithful will remain.*
> *Be still, my soul: thy best, thy heavenly Friend...*
> *Through thorny ways leads to a joyful end.*
>
> *Be still, my soul: when dearest friends depart,*
> *And all is darkened in the vale of tears,*
> *Then shalt thou better know His love, His heart,*
> *Who comes to soothe they sorrow and thy fears.*
> *Be still, my soul: thy Jesus can repay*
> *From His own fullness all He takes away.*[157]
>
> *(Verses 1 & 3 from Be Still My Soul Hymn)*

---

157 Katharina Von Schlegal, *Be Still My Soul,* 1752

grey

an invitation to live fully, not merely survive

"Grief is like joy, it's not something to be fixed."

-C.S. Lewis

Grey skies descend like a thick woollen blanket over the rolling hills, as if to tuck them in for the coming winter. There is no sunshine here. And with these clouds, I can't even see the North Star.

It's not yet cold enough for snow, the covering that somehow makes sense of late autumn's lifeless terrain and bitter winds.

Once again, the trees are near bare and as the temperature drops, I feel my own self submitting to the grey, to the need to be still, tucked in, reflective.

There is nothing I can do to make the clouds go away. I don't know the way out of my own wasteland. In fact, I am not sure I am supposed to find my way out. I simply have a promise that that which is barren will once again be lush. The *how* is a mystery. And I suspect it runs the same course as a growing child. Slowly, slowly and then seemingly all at once, the adult emerges.

It is my third autumn here in Southland.

As temperatures drop, I remember clearly the first, antipodean autumn. I was trying to cope with my world being turned upside down by the new culture I found myself in. We arrived at the end of the New Zealand summer from our California winter. It was a cold 58 degrees Fahrenheit (15C) on the late winter day we boarded the plane to carry us away to our new home and it was the exact same temperature the day we arrived! The acclimatized locals consider this to be warm! When it doesn't get much warmer than the 70's (21C) all year round, 58 is a good average. But when you are used to it getting up to 110 degrees (43C), 58 degrees is cold!

I am fine with it being cold in winter. Winter is supposed to be cold. But to have cold weather in summer or fall has been an assault on my

129

senses. That first summer people would say, *"You're cold? Why, this is warm! Wait for winter!"* And I would feel the same distinct dread that would try to overcome me while pregnant with my first child when veteran mothers would tell me their labour stories; there was no backing out and I did not know what lay ahead.

I am amused to come across an early journal entry, a snapshot of my first winter here:

> *It is ALL white outside my window. The earth has been covered by a soft blanket of snow. And just like that, hope is here. It would seem as if there is a sudden blank slate, a fresh start, a merciful ground covering from the threatening and biting air of autumn. God covers us.*

It seems that, in theory, I knew that God's way was to cover us.

> *Even in the most dormant season, even in the coldest time of the year, warmth has arisen by this sudden overnight blessing. The world is abuzz this morning in our home. The kids are itching to explore this new frontier. Barely a bite to eat and jackets are whizzed on, sleds are whipped out and they are shooting down the hill in our front yard. I am witnessing dizzying spins, ecstatic laugher and extreme joy in such simple delights. Is this what you are after in us, God? "Unless we become like little children..." Their very lives are an act of trusting you. They live honestly before you, pouring out their fears, tears and most importantly their joys. They so quickly enjoy and revel in your creative ways. They don't question it. —Maybe I should get my work done first? —Maybe my clothes will get wet? They just know that this moment is here for them, right now, and accept it with great bliss. I outgrew this, I matured.*

> *Now, I understand that*
>
> *If I am to walk with you, God,*
>
> *I must grow*
>
> *Down.*

Perhaps crossing Antipodes is my means of growing down?

White comes in many colours. Hope arises in the blackest places. And all of sudden, hope can come just like the snow. I was speaking to my sister this week. Life was indeed bleak. Does God not keep his promises? Like the two fools on the road to Emmaus we lament, "but we thought you were going to be the one to save us, God." "We thought you were going to…You said you were going to…?" **How many of us who are believers find ourselves to be like Joseph? We believe in the dream he has given us and suddenly find ourselves on the** *back road there. Betrayal, slavery, imprisonment is not part of the top ten leadership principles to make yourself a better leader. But God knows how to form himself in us—infertility,* **infidelity, illness, death, betrayal, crisis. He knows how to** *fashion and form an understanding of His goodness into the backbone of our soul. He allows the enemy to try us. And the enemy whispers with vengeance, "God does not want you to be happy! God does not have good things for you! He is holding out on you!" And sometimes we would seem to have no choice* **but to believe it as things go from bad to worse. But as we fight and offer a sacrifice of thanksgiving before God, as we declare his goodness, even when we can't see it, he is forging His truth** *into the very core of our lives.*

I didn't have any idea of the forging I was about to undergo.

Are you forming yourself in me, God?

My sister's life is messy now. Anything that could go wrong has. And as we spoke on the phone there was still no sign of the promises God had made her. Amid all hell breaking loose, the longing for the baby that has yet to be nearly cripples her from being able to take another step forward. The crisp, unbearably black, cold air of autumn threatening winter is upon her. We cry together, pray together. She passes the phone to my brother so that I might speak with him. I am thinking, "God, where are you? Is there no hope anywhere?" And then, just like our overnight snowfall, came an unexpected cry in the background a few moments later. Was it crying, laughter? My sister seized the phone from my brother and blurted into the phone, "You are not going to believe this. I just took a test (the millionth over a

ten-year period) and it has two lines! It says, "I'm pregnant!"
The doctors had declared it impossible. God had other ideas.
Hope has come. Winter isn't gone, but a soft covering has given
a new canvas and outlook to appreciate the season. She is not
out of the hard places to walk, but like the snow, hope has
renewed and covered her spirit. And our hope is this "Nothing
is impossible with God." Blessed is the person who stands
believing that God will accomplish what he has said.

So, is that it? Is that what I have been learning—how to stand?

If so, landing in Antipodes has had a way of taking what I thought I knew and forging it into the very core of my being. Crossing through the very centre of the Rubix cube, the very heart of God Himself, has required me to make the arduous journey from my head to my heart.

Head to heart. My first winter.

How was I to know what the second winter would hold?

With the descending cold of the second autumn, I was trying to keep warm after the shock of my father's death. I drew strength from the bare and vulnerable trees standing tall and dignified during that second winter.

Now, once again winter is on my doorstep. My third winter.

I no longer fear its arrival like I did in the first year. Perhaps I have begun to realise the secret of standing is to accept an invitation to dance with the Giver of life's music wherever it leads. As I am learning to surrender control for trust, I have made friends with myself in the cold and sorrow. There is a level of acceptance and acclimation that has happened. I know what to expect now. My blood is thickening to become what this land requires. I am learning to embrace the shorter days and longer nights as a time for rest. Without the commercial extravaganza of lights and Christmas, winter here offers a time to just hunker down.

I reach for my One Year Bible and read:

"After a long time, in the third year..."[158]

---

158 1 Kings 18:2

And something within is acknowledged: Three years of being upside-down can feel like *forever*. It has been a long time.

Things are no longer black; the storm has subsided.

But the mist of the storm lingers; the grey hovers.

I think about storms.

The biggest tempest ever recorded is found in the book of Genesis when God allowed the earth to be flooded, wiping out all mankind but one man and his family. Noah was warned by God that the storm was coming and to prepare for it by building a giant ark. This storm he was warned about and prepared for lasted 40 days and nights. He was tucked away safe in the ark God had had him built.

And yet safety does not necessarily mean comfort.

I wonder:

Did anyone get seasick?

Did the stench of the animals threaten to overcome them?

Did the family get on each other's nerves being closed in such a small space?

What about personal hygiene?

It would be 150 days before the worst was over, before the flood waters began to recede. It would be ten months before even a window could be opened. The scripture says, ***"Then God turned his attention to Noah and all the wild animals and farm animals with him on the ship. God caused the wind to blow and the flood waters began to go down. The underground springs were shut off, the windows of Heaven closed, and the rain quit. Inch by inch the water lowered."***[159]

I wonder how slow an inch by inch recession might feel and I wonder if Noah knew God was attentive to him in that time that must have felt like forever.

On the day of stepping out to possess the land again, God put a rainbow in the sky; a magnificent promise of God's enduring love and grace for his people — just a glimpse of the multi-coloured, multi-dimensional

159 Genesis 8:1-3 (MSG)

133

God who loves to live in covenant relationship with us. Noah is blessed by God and told: *"You're here to bear fruit, reproduce, lavish life on the Earth, live bountifully!"*[160]

But after all that, after seeing God fulfil His word to Noah, 120 years after He told him to build the ark, after the storm, after the future promise, the blessing…then what? Everything that Noah knew prior to the flood would have been gone. The appearance of the earth would have changed, even the climate. Every house, store, town would have been obliterated. Every soul he knew, besides family, gone.

He must have marvelled in God's goodness and faithfulness to His spoken word to him. But I wonder, as time went by, did Noah ever falter in knowing how to live the promise, the blessing? Did he ever feel grief, maybe even survivor's guilt? Did he ever feel overwhelmed by having to start all over at 601 years old? Was his body fit to replant a vineyard, or did he have some aches and pains like I do in my forties?

Maybe? I read that the next story is Noah getting drunk off his grapes and laying in a naked stupor. Was the sample of his crops just so divine that he couldn't stop drinking? Or in the greyness did he decide to numb himself from all the conflicted feelings swirling inside of him?

Give strong drink to him that is ready to perish, and wine to those that be of heavy hearts.[161]

Sometimes in the grey our hearts can hang heavy, waiting for sunshine to penetrate the clouds. Are you still here, God? Where are you?

And no sooner do I ask that I am reminded of an ongoing conversation I had with God when I still lived in California and was out on my daily walks.

On a late spring day, I arose to walk early. As I began my walk on a Monday, I was absolutely overwhelmed by the awesomeness of the mountain-view before me. I spontaneously blurted out, "There you are, God! When I see these mountains, I feel as if I am catching a glimpse of your face!" In that moment, I felt the sacred invade my rather mundane life. I could feel the nearness of God and zipped through

---

160 Genesis 9:7 (MSG)
161 Proverbs 31:6 (AKJV)

my day; encouraged, renewed and strengthened by such a reverential moment with the God of the universe.

The following day, I awoke with great anticipation to see such sights and feel the nearness of God again. Instead, a layer of brown smog hung at half-mast and covered most of my view. Feeling a lesson coming on, I said, "Oh…so when I can't see you, God, it's because of the smog in my life!" I arrived home somewhat sombre and heavy of heart, confessing the smog in my life.

On the third day, I procrastinated getting out of bed, not too keen to repeat yesterday's walk and talk. Still, trying to be self-disciplined, I embarked on my third walk of the week. Much to my surprise the smell of impending rain was in the air (Fresno might get rain 3-4 times a year!). Massive clouds hung in the air and again covered my view. I thought, "Aha! I can't make clouds happen! Clouds are the work of the heavens." At this point, feeling quite desperate for the experience I had had on the Monday, I cried out to God: "Why would you hide your face deliberately from me? I understand when I sin and allow things to come between us…but the scriptures say you are faithful and just to forgive all our sins when we confess them to you. I expected a clearer view today. Why the clouds? Are you really for me? Do you really want to be known?

Then much to my surprise God answered me within my heart. He said, *"I would be known by you. When you can't see me, I am teaching you to hear me."*

"What if I can't hear you, God?"

"Then I will teach you to smell me."

"What if I can't smell you?"

"Then I will teach you to taste me."

"What if I can't taste you?"

"Then I will teach you to touch me."

"What if I can't touch you?"

"Do those mountains move?"

"No"

"Then you will rest in the knowledge that as sure as those mountains stand, so I AM. I will never leave you, nor forsake you."

It is comforting to think that perhaps in this present grey landscape of the soul, God is still here and as near as the Sierra Nevada mountains were during that week when I lost all visibility. And I wonder if I am learning more about Him than I can even fathom. Could these current clouds in my life be as a theatre curtain, which when pulled back might reveal something meaningful and creative between God and me?

Still, I am unsure—why the clouds? What do they represent?

"...the clouds are the dust of His feet."[162]

Excuse me, God?

"The clouds are the dust of 'MY' feet."

My memory is jogged and I run to find an old devotional by Oswald Chambers. Didn't he say something about clouds?

And sure enough, Chambers declares that clouds are the very evidence of God at work: "Clouds... *"are a sign that God is there. What a revelation it is to know that sorrow, bereavement and suffering are actually the clouds that come along with God!"*[163]

If that is so, these grey skies are a sign that help has come. This greyness I am experiencing indicates that the worst of the storm is over. Things are no longer pitch-black. The deep darkness has been tinted by white, illuminated by divine light.

Did Noah figure this out?

Little is said after the incident of being found drunk by his sons. One scoffed at his father and shamed him to his brothers. The other two covered their father. Noah curses the son who scoffed at him and blesses the sons who covered him. All three of his boys go on to have lots of children, fulfilling the command to reproduce.

---

162 Nahum 1:3
163 Oswald Chambers, My Utmost for His Highest, (Tennessee, Thomas Nelson, 1992), July 29

The scriptures simply state that Noah lived another 350 years following the flood, making it a grand total of 950 years, before he died.

It doesn't read like much of a conclusion.

But in light of the grey, it may be more significant than I could have ever seen before.

It says that Noah *lived*.

I realise that one can be alive and not really live.

Did Noah find a way to be present, to be sober, to live in the moment? Did he indeed learn to bear fruit, reproduce, lavish life on the Earth and live bountifully?

I feel a challenge to my soul.

How then shall I live?

beauty

an invitation to examine our source of identity

"This concept of beauty falls far outside our traditional understanding. But for Vincent, beauty was truth-telling first and foremost. Like a wound slowly healing, beauty was the outward proof of regeneration."

-William Havlicek

I have been contemplating this challenge to live.

I don't want to merely exist. I want to live.

I want to live what God has ordained for us: ***"You're here to bear fruit, reproduce, lavish life on the Earth, live bountifully!"*[164]**

I realize it's what I have always wanted. Maybe that's what we all want.

Maybe it's this longing that compels me to see the little beauties on the clearance rack. Splendid blooms of red and white extend out and past their 12 pack cartons. They are stretching, reaching, bursting with colour in this... their final season.

These annuals are on clearance. 12 packs marked down from $7.99 to $1.99. The market says their time is up. I look them over, root bound with some scraggly bits to be pinched off. I know they will not live past winter, but for **HOPE**...

The eyes of this amateur gardener think them worthy to bring home to **LIVE** in these final days. Up and out of the cartons they come. I group them with others into larger pots and stick them in my window box. There they rest, a colourful array, lifted up for all to see.

And they speak without words.

Faces upturned toward the sun,

> ...point the way to their TRUST in their last hours.

---

164 Genesis 9:7 (MSG)

Such Beauty, graciously reminding me to turn my face to the Son, to Trust and LIVE!

"Teach us to number our days aright, that we may gain a heart of wisdom."[165]

***

Beauty overwhelms and connects all synapses, calling forth that which would be remembered.

I see again my father's frail frame ravaged by the ferocious appetite of the cancer in his body. He had become root-bound, scraggly.

In my memory, the natural doctor tried to help. Pills, pokes and puffs of bright light were attempted to heal him as he lay on the table.

I held his hand in a superior position. My hand was on top of Dad's, trying to lend him courage.

The doctor said to me, "You'll need to cover your eyes with this laser treatment."

I buried my head into my father's side.

The light exploded into my darkness and in that moment, I suddenly felt as if I was five years old, not forty. And I remembered yet another deeply buried memory; *the feeling of sticky things all over my head as I laid on a cold, hard table, fearful for when the bright lights would start. The lights always took me and soon there would be nothing until I awoke.*

My body winced at the memory.

I muttered as my father underwent his treatment, "This feels like when I had my seizure treatments."

And another kind of beautiful light blasted onto the scene, that of CONNECTION, deep, true and holy, forged by a common bond of suffering.

"Now if we are children, then we are heirs-heirs of God and co-heirs with Christ, if indeed we share in his sufferings in order that we may also share in his glory."[166]

---

165 Psalm 90:12
166 Romans 8:17

My dad understood now in his suffering something that had been deeply buried within the heart of this little girl.

In a split second, the moment begged to be understood, cherished.

Dad responded, connected to my girl's heart by removing his hand from underneath mine and placing it on top. Even at his weakest moment, he was still my dad.

And the memory of this now pierces my spirit at some greater level. There is a truth to be grasped: The FATHER'S love, God's love, is always strongest and it always wins out!

Together, Dad and I held courage. No matter how brave our attempts were to hold onto God in this storm, God's grip has been stronger and His love, deeper.

The image of the golden wheatfield dancing, bowing to the wind, is before me again. And I understand that together we yielded to the dance of life in hope of glory.

Root-bound: There was nowhere else for Dad to grow in earth's container.

Scraggly—like the Velveteen Rabbit—life had rubbed off his nose and fur.

But his spirit burst forth in the end...PURE, FREE & STRONG.

LIVE he did—more gloriously in the end than in all the moments before.

And he spoke of HOPE beyond here. Hope in seeing his Jesus face to face.

And he prayed for his children. What did he pray in his half-delirious state for me?

"Help her, God, not to let the little foxes spoil the vine."

I thought it was a strange prayer, maybe a side effect of the morphine. But there it is written in black and white on the pages before me from the Ancient Holy Book:

"Catch for us the foxes, the little foxes that ruin the vineyards, our vineyards that are in bloom...My lover is mine and I am his..."[167]

---

167 Song of Solomon 2:15

Dirty laundry begs washing, weeds demand pulling, spilt milk on countertops needs cleaning and I think of all those little things that can happen in a day to steal our joy.

I growl at the kids when they won't get out of bed. And get cross with my man when he calls with another secretarial need. And I wonder why I allow potential special moments for connection to be disrupted.

And I wonder how I let the small stuff make me question the Almighty.

I look up, glance out and see those glorious blooms gently waving in the wind. They whisper on the wind...

"Consider you're an annual with only one life to live."

Live! Live! Live!

***

And as inspired as I am by the little red beauties, I wonder, how do I live the inspiration?

Is there *really* a way to live and not merely survive?

I know what it is to just be going through the motions. And there seems to be endless sources of advice on how to wake up and participate with life. There are countless shows, books and demos on how to *suck the marrow* out of life.

Just a pinch of an ancient aromatic spice to the chicken promises a form of ecstasy in the kitchen.

Restoration of an old piece of furniture can suddenly become a public declaration of the authentic self.

Climbing Mount Everest makes an adventurer.

Home-grown vegetables in a basket lend an air of pure organic living.

Fortune 500 clubs promise power, prestige and money.

Choosing to breast feed makes a very dedicated mother.

But in the grey, I still just feel numb.

All my previous striving seems vain.

141

Mary Oliver's instructions to live life are: "Pay attention. Be astonished. Tell about it."[168]

I haven't paid attention. The goal has just been to get out of bed every day and put one foot in front of the other.

Astonished? More like disillusioned.

Tell about it? Yes indeed! Complaining has become an art form for me.

I understand that I have been 'stuck'.

I ask God, "Why have I been stuck?"

And a quote that I just read comes to mind: "The strategy of evil is to attack your vision of the Father (God)."[169]

In the depths of my soul, I understand that I am still working out the character of this God that I believe in. But what does that have to do with enjoying the moment?

"How can you enjoy the moment when you don't know who I am?"

I don't understand.

"Identity, provision and protection come from me. You will never be free to enjoy the moment without these in place within you, otherwise, you will look to the moments to define who you are, or fill you up, or protect you…rather than just enjoy them as they are."

Well, then, what blocks me from receiving your identity, provision and protection, God?

'Sin'

O God! Sin??? I hate that word. It is so religious.

Google defines sin as *"any act regarded as such a transgression, especially a willful or deliberate violation of some religious or moral principle."*

Reluctantly, I ruminate on sin.

---

168 Oliver, Mary. https://www.goodreads.com/quotes/62038-instructions-for-living-a-life-pay-attention-be-astonished-tell
169 C. Baxter Krueger, *Across All Worlds: Jesus Inside Our Darkness*, (Jackson, Perichoresis Press, 2007), 75.

I was taught that sin means missing the mark, that it separates us from God.

And even though I know that Jesus died for my sins, I somehow internalized this truth as *I must make amends, try harder, be better.* For the perfectionist in me, it has made me try all the harder to get things right.

In short, I have understood sin to mean bad behaviour.

Not too long ago, one of my close friends made a confession to me that left this goody-two-shoes reeling. She confided, "I don't believe in sin. I think it's an antiquated idea made up by a medieval society to make everyone conform and stay in line."

At first, I wanted to dismiss her thought altogether. But her words would not leave me. One glance at church history proves an element of truth to her statement. Something needed to be examined. I considered her words long and hard. What if we just removed the constraints that the church is so notorious for putting on people? What if all rules and ideas of sin were removed? Would society suddenly become better? Would people become more selfless, loving and confident? Would big sins like murder and small sins like telling a white lie cease to exist?

Perhaps my Christian worldview confines me, but I cannot see this bringing life. Instead I find another question rising within me. What if sin is not merely a behaviour, but rather a condition? For even if all constraints, rules and ideas of sin were removed: would it eradicate fear, loneliness, shame, jealousy, bitterness and so on? What if bad behaviour is only symptomatic of a greater darkness manifesting in humankind? A darkness that haunts humans with aloneness, brokenness and whispers in its own way, *"You are not good enough, you are not acceptable, you are not important!"*

What if that is why Jesus died? What if he came to pierce that kind of darkness inside of me with *hope for more?*

Maybe the *greyness* is an indicator that light has come. But perhaps this light also illuminates— *highlights,* where the darkness still lurks inside the places that feel unacceptable, unlovable and unimportant.

highlights

an invitation to freedom

"The good news of Jesus Christ is not that we have an accurate religious manual to follow and a master leader to show us the way. And it is not that we finally have perfect information about God to learn. The gospel is about Jesus himself. He knows the Father. And the gospel is about the stunning fact that the Father's son has established a real relationship with us in our darkness. And in this relationship, he is sharing with us—with the world –his own mind and knowing, his own communion with his Father, forever."

-Baxter Krueger

I am not keen to have my darkness highlighted. Is anyone?

I pause and hear a familiar recording begin in my head. And I am quite shocked at what God seems to be highlighting.

The *Shoulds* within my head start to scream at me. Like an abused child, I lower my eyes; stand quietly, hoping it will pass. But the screams are just a warmup. In my weakness, the *Shoulds* know how to work me.

PUSH!

Look at this DIRTY KITCHEN SINK! Why can't you keep it SHINY AND DISH FREE?

SHOVE!

DO YOU REALISE HOW FAR YOU ARE GETTING BEHIND YOUR DAILY ROUTINE? WHAT ABOUT THE GARDEN, THE FIRE, THE ANIMALS, THE GARAGE, THE BILLS?

There is no sympathy or understanding. They don't care that I had a speaking engagement on Friday night, a massive sit-down dinner to host on Saturday night, a husband who had to speak at church on Sunday, a grieving high school girl to comfort on Sunday evening, school pictures to have my kids ready for this morning…

SLAM!

And now they are attacking my appearance. I need to work out more. My chin is doubling. I am aging.

And I agree.

I am aging. My chin is doubling. My weight at 40 years is higher than at the age of twenty.

I can see that all the things the *Shoulds* mentioned need to be done. And I try. But they are never satisfied. And just as I tick off the last of my 'to-do' items on my list, new accusations of selfishness and vanity are hurled into my mind.

"YOU ONLY CARE ABOUT YOURSELF! YOU SHOULD HAVE CALLED SO-AND-SO BY NOW! YOU ARE CONCERNED ABOUT TRIVIAL THINGS! DON'T YOU KNOW THAT THERE ARE CHILDREN IN THIRD WORLD COUNTRIES WHO ARE DYING FROM HUNGER AND ALL YOU CARE ABOUT IS THAT YOUR CHILD IS GETTING THE RIGHT NUTRIENTS???"

Confusion sets in. All my values have turned on each other.

I don't want to feel powerless. And so I do what I know to do. I start to run, the *Shoulds* still with me. I run and run—their whips at my feet, until I fall weary into my bed. And still, it's not good enough! Nothing is ever good enough for this… *spirit.*

With the word *spirit,* I am jarred conscious, awake.

"Now where the Spirit of the Lord is, there is Freedom."[170]

Freedom? *O yes please!*

And I suddenly see that this spirit of the *'Shoulds'* is not of God!

I imagine this invisible force against me and am shocked by what I see. The brute forces behind the tyranny I have experienced are not what I thought. They look like little tiny gargoyles dressed up as monks. Their job is to nip at my heels.

They are small enough that I could…step on them.

---

170 2 Corinthians 3:17

"I have given you authority to trample on snakes and scorpions and to overcome all the power of the enemy; nothing will harm you."[171]

The *'Shoulds'* scurry away to get the master of their presumably righteous order and I know I have minutes before the inquisition will begin.

The shapeshifter arrives, looking almost like Jesus, but for the eyes.

"...Satan himself masquerades as an angel of light."[172]

He looks good, proper, religiously clean—but for the eyes, cold and calculated.

And then he speaks, his words patronizing: "Now, now, we have done this before. You have been great before and if you work just a little harder, you shall remain great."

This shapeshifter trying to look like Jesus is asking me to go back to being religious about my Christianity, my body, my home, my children, my marriage. And for a second, I waver. It all looks so good, so right. But I know that there is no life in religion, only lists to accomplish, tense shoulders from burdens not meant to be carried, fatigue, even death.

"Come to me, all you are weary, I will give you rest."[173]

The voice of the true Master contrasts with that of the imposter. The true Jesus didn't come into the world to condemn but save. I reach for the lifeline He throws to me.

"...The great triumph is not in your authority over evil, but in 'My' authority over you and presence with you. Not what you do for 'Me', but what 'I' do for you – that's the agenda for rejoicing!"[174]

And I realize afresh, "All my righteousness is as filthy rags."

Amazing Grace

How Sweet the Sound

That

Saved a Wretch Like Me[175]

---

171 Luke 10:19
172 2 Corinthians 11:14
173 Matthew 11:28
174 Luke 10:19-20 (MSG)
175 William Wilberforce, *Amazing Grace*, 1779

146

Grace isn't just for overt sinners, it's also for the ones who have grown weary of trying so hard to do everything right.

I see. My blinders are off.

I didn't realize that I was controlled by these voices. That I allowed myself to be regularly battered by their demands. Why?

Lord?

I recall the flashes of light again when Dad was undergoing his treatment, triggering vague memories from the five-year-old girl in me. She helps me to remember the original *lights*.

I would have to put on a hospital gown with the encouragement and help of my mother. The doctor would tell me to "Climb up onto the table." It was cold. The lights were turned on and the machine would begin to hum a left to right whirring beat. An unspoken chant would resound in my brain, each word pronounced slowly to the back and forth rhythm: – Something –Is –Wrong –With – My –Brain. I was told to stare at the light and then there would be nothing as I gave way to sleep. I'd awake, get dressed, be handed stacks of colouring paper (computer paper that tracked my brain waves) and a jellybean.

I didn't understand, not really.

I told my four-year-old sister that she would have to be the big sister after I died. She regressed to bed-wetting. If she didn't grow up, I couldn't die.

But still I tried to be brave. I was a good little girl who could swallow a big person's pill with a glass of water.

I started school that year. I tried to do well in school. But I couldn't seem to stay awake with the phenobarbital in my system. I was no match for the heavy barbiturate drug that slowly drained my personality, memory and ability to stay present.

I failed first grade.

And as I say it, I can feel something churn in my gut, a hint of my buried shame.

My mother said she caught the little boys chasing me home with sticks in their hands, waving them in my face and teasing me, *"First grade baby! First grade baby!"*

Even now, I can feel a small part of me raise up her chin defiantly and say, "I will never fail again!"

She didn't, I didn't.

After a year, two church ladies who had been praying for me at our church came to my mother and said, "We think God has healed Sarah. You should take her off the medicine."

So, Mom inquired of the doctor, "Could we begin to reduce the medication to see how she does?"

Slowly I improved until I was completely weaned off. I not only caught up to my normal grade, I excelled. I excelled so much that I would get upset with myself if I even got an 'A minus' on a report card. I could and I would prove that I was acceptable.

Quite suddenly I understand why I have listened to the *Shoulds*. It has worked for me. I excelled, succeeded. Under their direction, I became successful, beautiful, popular.

And now all at once, I come face to face with my own sin: *pride.*

Like the witch from Snow White, I have known power from all kinds of beauty. And like the Pharisees of Jesus' day, I fear losing my power and place as they have been essential to my survival.

"Time's up! God's kingdom is here. Change your life and believe the Message." [176]

Jesus' words in the Gospel of Mark penetrate my thinking and I feel the crux of a deep question in me.

Believe? Believe what message, God?

I read another version: "Repent, the kingdom of God is at hand."

Repent?

------

176 Mark 1:15

I have learned that *repent* means to literally turn and face the other way.

In order to turn, don't you have to know what you are turning from and what you are turning towards? Obviously, Jesus wants us to turn away from something towards the kingdom of God. But what does that actually mean?

If I am being asked to turn away from my pride, to embrace the kingdom of God, what does that look like?

My head understands the concept, but I don't know how to actually work this out in my life. How do you embrace an invisible kingdom?

I try to read for any other clues, but Mark doesn't elaborate on the sermon. It's as if we are to understand by the preceding events why Jesus would just stand up and begin to tell people to repent. I examine the scriptures before it; there is the announcement of John the Baptist as a forerunner for Christ, John baptising Jesus, Jesus being tested in the desert and then the beginning of Jesus' preaching: ***"Change your life and believe the message."***[177]

God?

My eyes lock on the blessing God pronounces on Jesus at his baptism.

"You are my Son, chosen and marked by my love, pride of my life."[178]

God, the king, gives His fatherly blessing.

Well obviously, it's his son, Jesus. What does that have to do with me?

And the question that rises within me feels radical: If Father God is the creator of all things, is he not our father too? Is that same blessing meant to be for me? Is it meant to be embraced?

Do I see myself as a beggar or a princess? Beggars behave very differently than princesses.

What is Jesus asking me to believe and turn towards?

Before 'original sin' could there actually be an 'original blessing?'

---

177 Mark 1:15 (MSG)
178 Mark 1:11 (MSG)

I recall the words of a dear friend processing the broken pieces of his own life. In his brokenness and poverty, he had found a treasure of great worth. Humility poured off him as only it can when one has hit rock bottom and grabbed hold of God. And he spoke of this verse as if it were an anchor for his life. With a deep quiet on him, a deep peace, he spoke of these words and said, "Do you realize that God spoke a blessing over Jesus before he had ever done anything noteworthy? Jesus hadn't yet preached, healed, loved or died. And yet God announced His deep pleasure in him."

This friend, once a pastor, continued to share how he had spent his whole life trying to serve God with a frenzy. It wasn't until his wife left him that he hād to take a long hard look at his choices. He couldn't understand her pleas to slow down, be present, to speak kindly to their children and to see her. He just kept on trying to meet the demands of his parishioners. He was blind because he didn't know that he was still trying desperately to gain his father's approval; an impossible task, as his father was dead. He didn't know he was still trying to gain the affirmation he had always longed for, but never received. He didn't know he was striving to hide the emptiness and shame of his youth and was desperate not to fail.

It would seem that he had lost everything when she left. He had failed. But in his failure, God had met with him and declared His blessing over him:

"You are my son, chosen and marked by my love, pride of my life. Turn and believe this message!"

Our friend was a changed man, inside out.

Has the invitation always been to receive, to believe that the Father has marked us with his love, that we are the pride of his life, should we choose to embrace it?

Are you asking me, God, to turn from my pride, my self-made ways and embrace that I am your daughter, chosen and marked by your love, the pride of your life?

My spirit resonates with this. My head understands. But there is a battle within.

Am I willing to turn from all my self-made ways? They have served me well for over forty years.

And the Imposter's words suddenly echo ancient words. It is repackaged, but with the same meaning:

"All this I will give you, if you bow down and worship me."[179]

And it could be done. I could literally bow down by trying harder. I feel the temptation for such glory.

And then I read the words of my master…

"Away from me, Satan! For it is written: 'Worship the Lord your God and serve him only."[180]

The *Shoulds* clamour loudly for my attention. They are thieves, looking to steal my worship from the one true God.

Forgive me, God! I do believe, help my unbelief!

I declare the words of the Master: *"Away from me, Satan!"* For it is written: Worship the Lord your God and serve him only."

And something happens…

I remember.

I remember my mother's voice telling me how that evening after the boys chased me home, that she found me crying in my bed. Apparently, my father had read the Bible that evening. The story had been about Jesus being beaten by the soldiers, jeering and mocking him before they crucified him.

My mother asked me, "Sarah, honey, what is the matter?"

She said that I replied, "I didn't know, Mommy!"

"What, Sarah? What didn't you know?"

"That they treated Jesus that way too!"

And in this moment, the soldier's jeers, *"King of the Jews! Ha!"* mixes with my own shame, *"First grade baby!"*

The truth that God has been teaching me is moving in.

---

179 Matthew 4:9
180 Matthew 4:10

Jesus didn't just die for my sin—my pride— so I could be a better person. He went deeper. He endured my shame, my loneliness, my fear, all my darkest places so that I might know that I am not alone and that there is hope and freedom.

God grew down; He humbled Himself to love.

This is not a God who turns away from us when we turn from Him. No, he stays fixed, shining His light on our back should we turn away. Are not the very shadows that we fight evidence of this?

Sin may keep me shadow-focused and unable to see Him, but God never leaves, never stops loving. If Christ died before the creation of the world, then a plan and way to keep us connected has always been in place. He has done the work to close the gap, all I must do is turn around.

"Repent! Turn around and look at me!"

No condemnation? No trying harder to get things right? No beating myself up? No need to do penance? Am I really just to turn around and let His arms enfold me— choose to live from that place of embrace?

I am brought back full circle, another level deeper and more intimate, that this is a God who wants to walk with me, no, to love me, not only in my light, but also in my darkness.

Once again, I can feel the Son beaming down on me, smiling.

"There is no failure here, sweetheart!"

Once again, a smattering of phrases burst onto the window of my soul:

"If God be for us, who can be against us?"[181]

"There is no condemnation for those who are in Christ Jesus."[182]

"Perfect love casts out fear..."[183]

"Therefore, I will boast all the more gladly about my weaknesses, that Christ's power may rest on me."[184]

---

181 Romans 8:31
182 Romans 8:1
183 1 John 4:18
184 2 Corinthians 12:9

sunshine

an invitation to embrace life in all its ups and downs

"Joy is the serious business of heaven."

-C.S. Lewis

It seems that I have been on a spiral path. There is a springing forward, a looping back around, before curling forward again. I think I have learned something, only to loop back and re-learn or implement the thought again, to re-establish what I have learned. Presently, I am back in California to help my mother move out of her great big house into a smaller, modest cottage at the beach. Time will tell if I am curling forward or back this round.

I feel only joy sitting on the outdoor patio with the bright coloured chairs and table umbrellas. The temperature is perfect, not a hint of that cold wind that likes to permeate my bones down under. I have a lunch date with Betty, my silver-haired friend and sage.

Betty is a nickname for Elizabeth. And as I write this, my memory suddenly takes me back to the Christmas morning our newborn daughter, Elizabeth Grace Noel, was laid in my arms. *Grace promised of God.*

Once again, I look into a face that means *"promise of God."*

And I wonder, what kind of promise?

Are you one to keep your promises, God?

"These were all commended for their faith, yet none of them received what had been promised."[185]

And even as I write the question, I wonder what I'm really trying to ask?

So, I focus my attention back to the moment, back to Betty.

Here I feel peace, warmth.

---

185 Hebrews 11:39

If the Holy Spirit had a body, I can't help but think that this divine spirit might disguise itself as Betty. She carries a beauty of one who knows herself and is comfortable in her own skin, so that I'm often not even aware of her seventy plus years. There is a perpetual twinkle in her eyes that communicates without words that *all is well and shall be well.* It comes from a deep spring within her of believing that she is known, loved and accepted by Father God.

Like the Holy Spirit who loves to reveal Jesus, Betty loves to talk about Jesus. But it is always completely absent of any hint of religion. I am not even sure if she brings His name up, but it is as if He is right there with us. And since Jesus loves to reveal the Father, it is as if having time with Betty is like having lunch in a deep sacred circle of love. And I feel that I am loved, known and accepted not for anything I have done, not done or am doing…but simply because it's the way it has always been. And I wonder if this isn't why Jesus, before the foundations of the world, died for our sins— that we might live within this everlasting circle of love between the Father, Son and Holy Spirit?

Her eyes crinkle with laughter as she informs me that she is buying lunch and that she thinks we should order half a glass of wine each to have with it. What I really hear her saying is, "Let's savour and celebrate this moment." And for a moment, I find rest and strength in her joy.

And no sooner do I write this than I hear, ***"The joy of the Lord is your strength."***[186]

I have always thought that I had to have more joy, so that I could be strong. But how then can I be weak and strong? I have never considered resting in God's joy before, in His certainty, in His delight for the moment I am in.

But as I accept and enter into Betty's joy, I am at peace. And I feel a small light bulb switch on in my head. I am beginning to grasp Jesus' words in the context of this moment, ***"Take my yoke upon you."***[187]

Conversation between Betty and I flows. We have much to catch up on. We enjoy meandering in and out of each other's worlds and thoughts.

186 Nehemiah 8:10
187 Matthew 11:29

Out of nowhere, Betty says:

"You know what I have been thinking a lot about? This business in Ecclesiastes 3 that says there is a time for everything, EVERYTHING! Like, what does that mean that there is a time to gather stones and to scatter stones? And it's the conclusion in it all that is so interesting to me. The wise man finishes, *"I know that there is nothing better for men than to be happy and do good while they live. That everyone may eat and drink and find satisfaction in all his toil-this is the gift of God."*[188]

She takes a sip of her wine.

I consider:

There is a time for everything and a season for every activity under heaven:

> *A time to be born and a time to die,*
> *A time to plant and a time to uproot,*
> *A time to kill and a time to build,*
> *A time to weep and a time to laugh,*
> *A time to mourn and a time to dance,*
> *A time to scatter stones and a time to gather them,*
> *A time to embrace and a time to refrain,*
> *A time to search and a time to give up,*
> *A time to keep and a time to throw away,*
> *A time to tear and a time to mend,*
> *A time to be silent and a time to speak,*
> *A time to love and a time to hate,*
> *A time for war and a time for peace.*[189]

I note the concept of seasons and the play of opposites, Antipodes! And the thought that comes to me is that I have been interpreting the Sermon on the Plain through a lens of suffering. Until now I have only seen a mandate to follow Jesus even if it involves suffering. I have understood that to follow Him is to choose the way down, not the way up; and I have believed that He is leading me, positioning me to encounter His Kingdom through this upside-down journey. But what if

188   Ecclesiastes 3:12-13
189   Ecclesiastes 3:1-8

155

I also need to interpret this journey across Antipodes through the words of this ancient Ecclesiastical philosopher as well? His admonitions to *eat, drink and be merry* seem almost hedonistic. Suddenly I find that I am holding a tension between what would seem to be polar opposites: the way of suffering and the way of pleasure.

I return to Ecclesiastes 3 and note the verse that follows; at once, I am paying attention:

"He has made everything beautiful in its time."[190]

What if God allows us to experience opposite seasons to encounter Him and the beauty that only He can bring? What if he allows us these experiences so that we truly learn that our identity, provision and protection are in Him and Him only, so that we are free to live, to enjoy the moments of just eating, drinking and enjoying our work?

Lunch is over.

The warm Californian sun kisses our skin as we walk along the creek up to the San Luis Obispo Mission. Betty wants to look at the Mission's bells I had told her about years ago.

I had forgotten.

There are three bells in a row out in the courtyard.

On the left is a bell named JOY. It is 25"in diameter, weighs 279lbs and plays C#.

The bell on the far right is slightly larger. Its name is SORROW. It is 26.5" in diameter, weighs 330lbs and plays E.

However, between Joy and Sorrow lies the largest bell. With a diameter of 28," it outweighs the other two bells at 476lbs.

Its name: GLORY.

I remember.

Hmm, a bit of a theme.

Like Moses, have I not been asking, 'Now show me your glory?"

---

190 Ecclesiastes 3:11

Again…what kind of glory???

***

Millions of diamonds glisten as the sun's rays light the frosted treetops, hedges and ground. I'm back here down under. It's magical to watch, even if I am struggling to keep warm. I have already reloaded the fire four times with wood and my nose is still frozen. And just as I complain of my chilled nose, the sun moves almost in response and hits me right between the eyes. Its brightness forces my eyes closed and in my temporary blindness, I am overwhelmed by the warm sensation upon my forehead. It seems to be softening the crease that has etched itself between my eyes.

A song plays: its beauty begs a name. I can't help but smile when I look to see the title, *New Life.*

Hmm.

And something else freezes, not in the way of being cold, but in the way of being suddenly still. There is something *glorious* in this moment to be absorbed.

Glorious: *illustrious, splendid, magnificent, delightful, enjoyable*[191].

I give way to it, the extraordinary in the ordinary. Sometimes life affords a glorious glimpse of beauty in the mundane; for a moment all seems right and I feel alive, intensely alive. Maybe it's due to such opposite extremes in temperature; I am cold, but the sun is so warm on my face that all my nerves and electrical impulses are jolted awake.

I glance up, survey my indoor surroundings and it's as if I can see Dad sitting on the couch our first Christmas here, like it was yesterday. His face alive by this same magic I now feel; His eyes brimming with tears of sheer joy as we cleaned up the Christmas wrapping paper to an Italian song playing on the stereo. We were being goofy as we did our chores, everyone singing along in their best Italian opera voices.

I revisit the song and note that its name in Italian is: *Ven a Mi.* I search for the English translation and it has only one word: *STAY.* The lump

---

191 Thesaurus.com, 'Glorious,' accessed October 12, 2019, https://www.thesaurus.com/browse/glorious?s=t

that seems to have taken up permanent residency in my throat begins to rise. That moment is gone. It could not stay. Dad could not stay.

How many moments in life I wish I could keep!

Perhaps I am only feeling nostalgic today, longing for the past. Did I value that moment with Dad when I was in it as I do now? I know I was happy, but I didn't know that it would be our last Christmas together. Would I have stopped or absorbed the moment more somehow had I known?

Walking in grief sometimes feels like walking down a very long corridor. A tear bounces out like a ball and rebounds back and forth off the walls, echoing sounds from long ago and sometimes a hint from the future not yet recognizable.

This current tear of beauty seems to echo other such moments of sheer joy: hanging upside down from the swinging monkey bars, falling asleep on my daddy's chest, the electric shock that went through my whole body the first time my husband held my hand, the overwhelming love when my firstborn was laid in my arms...

In hindsight, how fast eighteen years have flown by since my baby girl was laid in my arms! But in the day of small things, sometimes time just felt as if it were creeping by. How often in the midst of the chaos had I longed for merely a moment to myself? But now, she too, the firstborn is gone. She graduated from high school and flew the nest just last week. And is that not what grief really is: What or who we once held tight in our arms is no longer ours to hold?

It has been said that we don't know what we truly have until it's gone. It is easy to take life for granted. And I realize that I keep looking for a way to live my life without any regrets. I want to live with my eyes wide open, not missing any more moments—but how?

Even now a funny kind of guilt consumes me when I try to resolve not to miss any more moments of life, especially with my loved ones. Did I not just this very morning eagerly wait for my family to leave so I could write? Is it even humanly possible to cherish every moment? As humans we get tired, we feel sad, bored, hungry, angry, thirsty...

*"Blessed are you who weep **now**."*[192]

There is a jarring in my soul when I hear the word 'Now', a sudden movement like my back being put back into place by one swift move from the chiropractor. I am left dizzy and wait for the ultimate effect.

A picture I once saw in a psychology book looms before my mind. Depending on how I looked at this drawing, I could either see a young woman or an old woman. I naturally only saw one image at first, until a friend pointed out another way to see it. My eyes had to readjust as I began to understand what she was seeing; it didn't negate the first image that I saw, rather, it added another dimension to the picture to appreciate. And like this photo, the eyes of my heart are trying to readjust to what Jesus is trying to get me to see. His words are taking on new meaning, another dimension to appreciate.

"Blessed are you who weep now…"

In this moment, this little diamond of scripture is being held up to the light of His presence. And I have never seen the angle in which these rays are streaming through the word *now*.

Now!

Blessed are you who hunger NOW, who weep NOW…

And I grasp that living present, seizing the moment, does not mean I have to create *'La Vie en Rose'*. It means embracing all parts of life, not just the picturesque pain free moments.

I am not sure where I gathered the idea that to enjoy life I had to create as many beautiful moments as I could, live certain and avoid sadness. But if Jesus blesses hunger and weeping NOW, then I am truly released to seize the moment. For even if the moment is negative, scary, sad, I can have the confidence that all things are made beautiful in His time. The present pain can become the fertilizer in life's soil that in turn produces lavish fruit.

What's an answer without a question? What's joy without sadness? What's peace without knowing unrest?

---

192 Luke 6:21

Until now, I have only understood Jesus' invitation in Luke to live in poverty, hunger, weeping and oppression as a means of obedience, of understanding God in his suffering, of counting the cost and making the sacrifice.

"Unless you pick up your cross and follow me."[193]

But at my lunch with Betty, I knew her question about the words of Ecclesiastes were poking at my dutiful grief and questions.

"I know that there is nothing better for men than to be happy and do good while they live. That everyone may eat and drink and find satisfaction in all his toil-this is the gift of God."[194]

What if Jesus' invitation to encounter poverty, hunger, weeping and oppression are actually a means of blessing. I don't mean God bestowing his blessing upon his subjects like a teacher handing out a math award.

But what if choosing to embrace life even in these forms naturally yields a blessed life, a *'joie de vivre'*? When I don't have to attempt to protect my own wealth, stress myself out trying to satisfy my deep empty places, be afraid of my own sadness and or what others might think of me, am I not then being released to find true freedom, satisfaction, beauty and joy?

Jesus' words ring an invitation to my heart to accept life *in all* its forms. To everything there is a time and a season. There is no guilt, no condemnation, just an appeal to let go and let Him work in my weakness, my lack of understanding, my fears and my sadness.

It feels like a slow death to encounter poverty, hunger, weeping thus far, but the promise to the end of "unless you pick up your cross and follow me" is "for whoever shall lose his life, will find it."

This is the ultimate invitation to REALLY LIVE NOW:

"Come as you are! Come breathe free!

And I will show who I am and you will know who you truly are.

I know how to take that which is dead and make it alive.

---

193 Mark 8:34
194 Ecclesiastes 3:12

I specialize in joy."

I remember again the bells that Betty and I saw on that glorious afternoon. I could feel the weight of their promise, as I can feel the sun's kiss now.

Glory!

I don't have to turn every moment into joy. Sometimes sorrow and pain are present and sometimes they can even weigh heavier than the moments of joy. But life surrendered to Him, life dependent on His joy, yields a *third way* rich with meaning, purpose and aliveness.

What was God's response to Moses again when he asked to see God's glory?

"I will cause all of my goodness to pass in front of you, and I will proclaim my name, the Lord, in your presence."[195]

Is that not what God has been doing? As Love has been moving into deeper places within me, bringing His goodness, am I not understanding the truth of who he is, his name being proclaimed in my presence?

With this revelation of glory, I see the greyness is breaking up, revealing patches of blue sky.

Once again, a drop of hope moves its way through to the depths of my soul.

I am being invited to trust that all is well and shall be well. Not just in my circumstances, but in me.

If God is the great *author and perfecter of our faith[196]* does He not know how to weave all the elements of our story into a masterpiece? What joy that must give Him. And it is in this, His joy, that I choose to find both rest and strength, before moving into the final frontier.

---

195 Exodus 33:19
196 Hebrews 12:2

op.pres.sion

1. the exercise of authority or power in a burdensome, cruel, or unjust manner.

2. the feeling of being heavily burdened, mentally or physically, by troubles, adverse conditions, anxiety, etc.

"Count yourself blessed every time someone cuts you down or throws you out, every time someone smears or blackens your name to discredit me.

What it means is that the truth is too close for comfort and that that person is uncomfortable.

You can be glad when that happens - skip like a lamb, if you like! - for even though they don't like it, I do. . . and all heaven applauds. And know that you are in good company; my preachers and witnesses have always been treated like this."

Luke 6:22-23

AFTERMATH YEAR FOUR:
DOES GOD DELIVER US?

fear

an invitation to let God walk us through fear

"The scariest monsters are the ones that lurk in our souls."

-Edgar Allen Poe

The greyness has indeed begun to lift. Where only mist, fog and cloud reigned over my vision, now clarity of shapes, colours and form are once again being seen. At first, I felt great joy, but as things have crystallized, I have been surprised by my latest emotion: fear.

I look for an analogy to grasp where I now am in my spirit.

In the mist, I could only and barely see the path right before my feet. But as the fog has lifted, I see my current location as walking along a very narrow cliff top and can see not only the slim path before me, the rocky wall to my left, but also the sheer drop to my right.

I am not sure I understand this analogy because where my feet are physically standing seems to be on ground with wide open space. I am blessed to live among green hills, fresh air, and skies that sing the most fantastical arias. Overall, the people are steadfast, humble and true. There is a level of safety and trust that I have never encountered in California: People leave their kids in the car when they run into the grocery store. Everyone watches out for their neighbour. Truly it's a lovely place; my dad when he saw it called it idyllic. But in my spirit, I seem to be aware of this narrow precipice I am walking, trying not to fall off the cliff. If I am honest, somehow, I feel threatened and as if I am constantly needing to look over my shoulder.

When I look for a word to describe this feeling, 'persecute' is what comes to mind. Again, that doesn't make sense. When I think of persecution, I think of Syrian refugees and nothing of my present circumstances would seem so dire. Nonetheless, I decide to look up the meaning for 'persecute' in hopes of gaining some understanding. The online thesaurus lists these synonyms; *bother, hound, harass, hunt, injure, molest, oppress, pester, pursue, worry.*[197]

---

197 Thesaurus.com, 'Persecute,' accessed October 12, 2019, https://www.thesaurus.com/browse/persecute?s=t

It's odd, but I do feel like I am being bothered, harassed, oppressed in my spirit. I just can't quite figure out where it's coming from and how it is having a hold on me.

In a private conversation under the cover of darkness last night, I confided in my husband. "Sometimes I feel such a heaviness come over me. I know this sounds weird, but it feels black and like it's trying to push my head backwards under water." He didn't know what to say, so he prayed for me. I slept like a baby, the sweetest sleep ever. I could hear prayers for me being muttered and I felt cradled as I rested. The peace was so immediate, so drastic, I thought maybe I was having a hormonal swing; my friends have warned me that this can get more intense at my age. But the next day, I felt a sudden urge to call one of my dearest friends back in California. She greeted me and before I could say another word, blurted out, "Sarah! Oh My! Janet (our other good friend) came over last night; I haven't seen her in months. We were sitting here talking when suddenly, we just started praying for you. It must have gone on for over an hour. There was this weird blackness around you, trying to push you back and under water?!"

I was dumbfounded! What I had whispered to my husband in private here in New Zealand, she was now telling me verbatim from California! Clearly, I wasn't imagining things nor was I having a hormonal imbalance. The Lord confirmed that there was a real force threatening me.

Evil is real.

I know the scriptures say that: *"the one who is in you is greater than the one who is in the world."*[198] In short, God is greater than any evil force.

"If God is for us, who can be against us?"[199]

If that is true, then why do I still feel afraid?

I brushed shoulders with overt evil at the age of twelve. Safety and security were shattered the day my classmate, Candace, was kidnapped. A sense of powerlessness and hopelessness set in when none of our efforts; flyers, search parties and prayers were successful in finding her, until it was too late. After six weeks of searching through the dead of winter across the land I grew up in, Canada's Midwest, they finally

---

198 1 John 4:4
199 Romans 8:31

found her tied up in a shack, frozen to death. And I wonder if I was the only student at that Christian school that felt my heart shackled with the news that day? Was I the only one whose soul was frosted by the enemy's lies: *God is indifferent, God is impotent, or better yet, God is dead!*

And yet I have decided that for me, in the fullness of time, lies born from blatant evil are easier to identify. Like old fashioned war, where two opposing sides line up and open fire, it is clear who the enemy is and where to aim. It's the other kind of evil, insidious evil, that makes me the most uneasy. Insidious evil is of an entirely different sort. It manifests more like terrorism; everything seems fine and then the bomb goes off.

Growing up as a pastor's kid, I have seen my fair share of these synonyms for insidious: *subtle, sneaking, cunning, crafty, artful, guileful, deceitful, deceptive, dishonest, duplicitous, false, like a snake in the grass.*[200] Perhaps my clearest memory of such behaviour was when I found and read a card on my father's desk. It looked benign, cute. A kitty cat was hanging by its claws off a tree branch. The inscription of the original card was supposed to bring a laugh:

"When things get tough, QUIT!"

But in the spirit of this insidious form of evil, this artful, underhanded card buzzed up our shirts and stung us with, 'We don't want you here!" There was not any handwriting in the card, only a Bible verse typed into it with the name "Anonymous" signed underneath it. And I couldn't help but wonder who sent it. Why the type? Was it a good friend? Why couldn't they come and talk to Dad? Were there others? And were they all talking together about Dad? What was the issue? These were the people who were supposed to be for us; I thought they were family, not the enemy.

It was a real sting, a welt appeared, but there was nothing obvious to swat at, there was nothing to target. Where then do we direct our anger? Seek justice? Who do we forgive?

---

200 Thesaurus.com, 'Insidious,' accessed October 12, 2019, https://www.thesaurus.com/browse/persecute?s=t

Insidious evil masquerades as light. It rarely confronts directly. It loves a messenger, a terrorist. Perhaps the greatest act of global terrorism that I have witnessed in my world was September 11, 2001.

At 6:48am, Dad had called and said, "Turn on the news!"

And there, my husband and I, each with a babe in arms, watched the horror of the twin towers crumbling before our very eyes. I could feel fear swirl around us, wondering what would happen next. Just hours before, around midnight, we had already encountered an explosion out West in our world. Dad had stopped over to our home after a board meeting to tell us that he had resigned from the church after seventeen years of ministry. We didn't understand, the church was at an all-time high. Things were more than fine on the surface, but underneath, the insidious evil was conniving its way.

Life in America changed after 9/11. Slowly daily life resumed, but fear had struck freedom hard in the face and she could no longer live with her heart wide open. America's freedom was hankered by the need to look over her shoulder, always watchful for the next attack. Coming and going through its boundaries became much more difficult and life lost a kind of golden innocence.

And as I write this, I understand that it wasn't just America that learned to live with walls around her heart.

God, that is the past! What does that have to do with here? With now?

I am met with a silent invitation to walk the narrow precipice, eyes wide open, through the final frontier of this antipodean journey to find the answer.

weakness

an invitation to a desert encounter

"My grace is sufficient for you, for my power is made perfect in weakness."

-2 Corinthians 12:9

When I search for clarity, all I get is static. Certainly, the S*houlds* are clamouring for my attention again. There seems to be an ongoing threat here to be useful or else. I feel compelled to do many things, good things for the sake of the Lord's work, but I know that the *Shoulds* are a poor substitute for life—and I am in need of life.

So in the dark, in the quiet, once again I ask: "Lord, where are you?"

And I can hear my heart echo my mind: "Lord? Where are you? I'm so weary. I have had enough, I just can't seem to get things right, I can't seem to embrace here, do enough, be myself. I am afraid."

At first, I see nothing. I only hear a phrase and recognize it echoes a scripture. ***"The journey has been too much for her."***[201]

Then I see myself laying limp, lifeless as a rag doll, on the ground. Jesus scoops me up, a heap of flesh off the ground into his strong arms and carries me to the Father. In the throne room, he lays me across Father God's lap. I lay there flat, unconscious, hopeless, like a set of tired old drapes. I watch the Father put his mouth to mine and blow. My thumb inflates, like a pool floaty, before the image ends, while something deep within me yields, accepts once again my weakness. It has been a long journey and there is more to go. Tears flow, cleansing my numbness, strengthening me to go the distance as I reach for my Bible to search for the verse in its context. There it is— 1 Kings 19:3-7:

"Elijah was afraid and ran for his life…when he came to Beersheba in Judah…he came to a broom tree, sat down under it and prayed that he might die. "I have had enough Lord," he said…then he lay down under the tree and fell asleep. All at once an angel touched him and said, "Get up and eat." He looked around and there by his head was a cake of bread over coals and a jar of water. He ate and drank

---

201 1 Kings 19:7

and then lay down again. The angel of the Lord came back a second time and touched him and said, "Get up and eat, <u>for the journey is too much for you.</u>"

I note the difference in the verbs of what I heard said to me and how the scriptures say it: "has been too much" versus "is too much." I keep wanting this whole journey across Antipodes to be a 'has been', not the ongoing journey that it still seems to be. I hear another passage of scripture, an exchange between Jesus and his disciples that seems to echo in the depths of me, revealing my heart.

"You do not want to leave, too, do you?"[202]Jesus asked his disciples.

Peter responds for them, for me: *"Lord, to whom shall we go? You have the words of eternal life."[203]*

My spirit knows there is nowhere else to find life. Still, in my soul, I identify with Elijah; I have been wanting to run for fear of my life. Is that the weariness, how to stay and believe with my spirit, when everything in my soul, my emotions, is telling me to run?

What are you after in me, God?

And then I remember…

Six months ago, I spoke at a women's retreat and I saw amazing things happen. But on Saturday night, as I stepped down from speaking and walked to the back of the room, I saw the eyes of one woman seething and I knew that I was about to walk into a brick wall. She did not feel like I did things the way they were supposed to be done. She was suspicious and sceptical of what we called the Holy Spirit working; one woman while in worship spoke in tongues amidst the singing, the drummer was drumming too loud in one song and even though I was building on my morning talk that had used ample scripture, I didn't use enough scripture in my evening talk.

Logically, I knew that this woman was from an Open Brethren background and that the woman who was speaking in tongues was from a Pentecostal background; both loved God, both knew him, just from different 'sides of the cube' so to speak. The beauty of such a weekend

202 John 6:67
203 John 6:69

168

where women come together from different Christian backgrounds is the opportunity to see God through someone else's lens, colour or side of the cube. Furthermore, I could understand where this Open Brethren woman was coming from. There was a time where I did not believe in the Holy Spirit working in such a way, I was afraid of it, of being led away from truth. It was a long journey in my life to begin to trust that the Holy Spirit wasn't going to lead me away from truth, but rather lead me into greater truth. But no matter how rationally I tried to approach the matter, inwardly I felt afraid, afraid enough to say that I would not be a part of the next retreat and afraid enough to withdraw from places I had occupied.

I return to the story of Elijah looking for understanding. What's going on here? And can it shed any light on my current state?

From what I can tell, Elijah has just experienced what every Pentecostal church dreams of; fire falling from heaven, rain being poured out over dry ground and supernatural strength to do the impossible.

My immediate thought is, 'I wonder if he felt tired?' I felt tired after *just* speaking at a women's retreat.

A past conversation with my father interrupts my thought process. A few years before, I had called him after speaking at a youth event. I was tired and yet I was trying to make some important decisions that I felt needed attention in that moment, so I had called 'My Captain'. He asked all about the night before; I told him that God had showed up but not in a way I had ever experienced as a teen and that in some ways it had scared me. As I gave the message, kids started to weep, some fell down, some tried to bolt from the room and some seemed to be in such a deep place of prayer that they didn't move from their place for almost 45 minutes during the ministry time; none of these things would have happened at the Evangelical church or camps I had grown up in.

Discerning my fatigue and doubt, Dad said, "Hon, do you remember the story of the woman with the bleeding issue, how she reached for the hem of Jesus' garment?"

"Yes…"

Teaching, he asked, "When Jesus turned around, what did he say?"

"Who touched me?"

169

He pressed further, "Why?"

"Because, he felt power shoot through him."

"Hon, it sounds like last night power went through you. This can make you physically tired. Never presume to move forward or make big decisions when you are tired. Now is the time to rest and let God refill you. Until he does, wait."

What then must Elijah have felt surge through him to call down fire from heaven to settle a dispute of worship between the prophets of Baal and the Almighty Yahweh, to see rain fall at his request after a three-year drought and then to suddenly have the strength to outrun a chariot for sixteen kilometres??? How does one come down off that kind of high, that kind of mountaintop?

Unfortunately, I don't get to see Elijah model the let-down period gracefully, instead I watch him run for his life. This man who seemed almost made of steel just moments before is suddenly afraid.

WHY???

I note the words written down on page 197 in my husband's little NIV Bible:

"So, Jezebel sent a messenger to Elijah to say, "May the gods deal with me, be it ever so severely, if by this time tomorrow I do not make your life like that of one of them." Elijah was afraid and ran for his life."[204]

Hmm. A messenger, a terrorist, attacks him when he is exhausted and overwhelmed. And the threat is not only real, it is worded as a curse, *"May the gods deal with me ever so severely..."*

Still, why does Jezebel's threat, even if a curse, bother him? It's as if her words to Elijah are as kryptonite to Superman. What soft spot does she hit? Do I have one?

I can't find out too much about Elijah's past. He shows up on the scene in Israel during the reign of one of its most evil kings and queens: Ahab and Jezebel. Elijah appears before King Ahab and warns him that there will be no rain unless Israel turns away from worshipping false gods. God then tells Elijah to hide and provides supernaturally for Elijah's survival during the next three years while the land is held

---

204 1 Kings 19:2

in dire straits with drought.

So far, so good. Nothing too alarming. An entire chapter is dedicated to the incredible ways that God cared for Elijah's needs. After some time had passed, God gives direction to Elijah to go back and present himself to Ahab, for God was going to bring back the rain. In his course of return Elijah encounters Obadiah, who is noted as a devout believer and a servant of the King. And then comes a tiny sentence that packs a major punch while describing Obadiah:

"While Jezebel was killing off the Lord's prophets, Obadiah had taken 100 prophets and hidden them in caves."[205]

It is unclear if Elijah already knew about this massacre or not. Did Elijah know any of these prophets? If so, how many? What if some of them were his best friends? Or what if some of them were family members— for we know that in those days the prophets travelled in each other's company? Did he have questions? Sure, he had seen some great miracles, but if God allowed Jezebel to kill his friends, what might God allow now? If God had not delivered them from her, what guarantee did Elijah have? Had Elijah had time to process his grief? He lived, they died…

I note that Jezebel's name means, 'Where is your prince?' Her prince, her god was Baal. In his fatigue, this insidious evil seems to scream at Elijah, "Where is *your* God???" When he comes down off Mount Carmel and is the most vulnerable physically, emotionally and spiritually, this evil seems to move through the messenger's words like a sting ray's tail whipping up and piercing his heart in the place of unsettled grief and questions. It would seem that before he can even process what's happened, he's running. Like the cries of a newborn overdue to eat, Elijah's visceral system seems to be activated. Having had four newborns, I note that a baby's visceral cries are designed to make a mama respond, to scoop up the baby in her arms and pull it close to her breast. But who will tend to a grown man? It's fight or flight time and Elijah's cries take the form of fast and wide strides into the Southernmost part of Judah, a desert land.

---

205 1 Kings 18:4

I wonder, what have I not yet processed that makes me vulnerable to the fear that seems to pursue me here? Why was that encounter with the seething eyes so frightening for me? Why did I run away just like Elijah? Why did I not think to rebuke the blackness trying to oppress me?

Elijah's running is the first recorded geographical movement that is not done at the Lord's command and some commentaries allude to this as a weakness in Elijah. I try to decide if this is good or bad. Was he disobeying God? Should he have stayed and fought, trusted in God?

I wrestle. Like Elijah have I failed to trust, stand? Or if I have been learning to dance, what kind of dance step is this? I do know that I have been struggling to embrace this place. Am I in sin? My fear grows greater, until the thought occurs, maybe *right or wrong* is not the point. Why do I always want to make things black or white?

Mark Holloway says, *"The enemy's goal is not to just inflict pain, but to keep us from hearing the voice of God."*[206]

What if that is the point? What if the point is that Elijah, in a terribly human moment, experiences a deep fear that grips him in such a way that he can't hear God's voice? And instantly I recall the face of my childhood Sunday school teacher, Jenny Savage, and hear her saying, *"Elijah was a man just like us..."*[207]

It echoes in my ears... *"a man just like us, a man just like us, a man just like us."*

I look up this echoing phrase on the online Greek lexicon and it translates; *to have a nature like us, to have passions like us, to have feelings like us.*[208]

I am strangely relieved to think that this great man of God had feelings just like me; not just the nice ones, but the black ones; fear, doubt, despair...

As adults we learn to control our visceral system. We learn to use words to express our fears, hunger and pain. And for the darkest places, we

206 Mark Holloway, *The Freedom Diaries: God Speaks Back*, (New Zealand, The Freedom Assignment Limited. August 2013)
207 James 5:17a
208 Biblehub.com, 'A man just like us,' James 5:17, accessed October 14, 2019, https://biblehub.com/greek/3663.htm

learn to cover. What if part of this journey in Antipodes is to bring me face to face with my deepest and darkest fears? What if God himself is leading me into this kind of... *desert*?

"Therefore, I am now going to allure her; I will lead her into the desert and speak tenderly to her. There I will give her back her vineyards and will make the Valley of Achor a door of hope. There she will sing as in the days of her youth..."[209]

209 Hosea 2:14-15

truth

an invitation to go the distance

"The truth is that, given enough time, life bestows its gifts, a drop at a time, if we can find the courage to stay open to the mysterious flow that is larger than any one event."
-Mark Nepo

I grew up believing that the truth could set me free and the truth meant the scriptures. Hearing and obeying the Word of God was the way to live. The Holy Spirit was acknowledged but not really given a place to lead; in fact, churches that listened to the Holy Spirit were deemed as given to emotional hype. I still believe that all scripture is God-breathed, but I have come to understand that first and foremost: Truth is a person. Jesus is the way, the truth and the life. He is the Word and it is the Holy Spirit who reveals Truth. And Truth always reveals Father God.

But when I stepped down off that stage and had that encounter that evening with the woman, I felt a deeper accusation and threat in my spirit. It whispered beyond her words to me: "You're a heretic!" And, "I am going to kill you just as I did your father!"

And so, I ran in my soul to the desert.

Elijah ran first to Beersheba and then on out into the desert where he collapsed under a broom tree. And there, the angel of the Lord tended to the grown man, like a mama with her hungry tired babe. Hmm... what's with Beersheba and broom trees, God? Is there something I am supposed to take from this?

I decide to do a little research.

The Retama Raetam, or the white weeping broom tree was a natural canopy of renewal as it was often used as a rest spot for weary travellers. The embers from its bark lasted a long time and its branches were soft and often used as a mattress. I note that, even though Elijah is afraid, he runs to a place where he can be refilled. That's not a bad idea, I consider going out of town; sometimes there is nothing like a journey to lend perspective. (I hear God laugh. I retort: *For the record, I was not thinking about this soul journey across Antipodes! I was thinking of a nice hotel in Queenstown with a spa!)*

But why does Elijah travel so far? Why Beersheba?

After a little more research, I discover that Beersheba means Oath-Well and that it was a special place in the history of Elijah's people. Abraham was the patriarch of Elijah's people, of Elijah's faith. Centuries before, Abraham had dug a well in Beersheba where he made a treaty with the King of Gerar and then settled there. After Abraham died, his son, Isaac, found favour with God and excelled in the land. Then the Philistines became jealous and stopped up several of Abraham's wells, filling them with earth. In time, his son Isaac re-dug the wells and then dug the Oath-well.

Although, it's an interesting fact of history, I still don't understand why Elijah ran there before he went on out to the desert and collapsed under a broom tree. I review the story and end up reading about what happened the night before Isaac dug this well of promise. The scriptures say that the Lord appeared to Isaac and reassured him with the same promise that He had given to his father Abraham:

"I am the God of your Father Abraham: don't fear a thing because I am with you."[210]

When Isaac and his men dug for the well the next day, they struck water; a sign of God fulfilling his oath to Isaac that He would indeed be with him.

Suddenly I understand what Elijah might have been seeking. If he ran to a place where God had been faithful to his ancestors; he has come to a place where he can remember the promises God had already fulfilled.

Is this how to be refreshed, renewed?

I consider God's faithfulness in my own life. Certainly, He fulfilled His word in bringing us to New Zealand, the miracle birth of my niece, Indigo Rain and the gift of being by Dad's side when he died. And although I am grateful and can see the hand of God in all of this, if I am honest, there is still some greater threat lingering within…

---

210 Genesis 26:24

I keep remembering my father laying there fragile, wilting and trusting God. I heard him pray the words of Mary regarding his health, *"May it be to me as you have said."*[211] My father seemed to have the same attitude of that of the Apostle Paul who penned while chained to a wall in prison: *"Yes and I continue to rejoice, for I know that through your prayers and the help given by the Spirit of Jesus Christ, what has happened will turn out for my deliverance."*[212]

Deliverance???

What kind of deliverance? I would have expected the Apostle Paul's words to be a prophecy of a future free of prison, not his execution. I would have expected deliverance to mean that Dad might live, or at the very least, some obvious good thing might come out of his death. I heard Dad preach often on Romans 8:28, *"And I know that in all things God works together for good those who are called according to his purpose."* [213]

Is this a spring of living water— a spring of deliverance?

If so, it is muddied. There hasn't been an obvious sign of anything good coming out of my father's death.

It feels like a long time since Dad died, it's been four years.

I wonder how deep Jezebel's curse dug in Elijah. Maybe beyond the question of God's faithfulness to him or his friends in his present state of grief lay a greater question?

I can feel one rising in me on his behalf.

Did Elijah wonder if God would remain faithful to His promise to Abraham, Isaac and Jacob, even if their children, the Israelites, lost their way? Sure, God had fulfilled his promises to Abraham in a greater measure after his death; he did father a great nation and this nation had inherited the land, but his offspring were now blowing it in Elijah's time. The great nation had divided into two and were violating their part of their covenant to walk with God and worship him only.

---

211 Luke 1:38
212 Philippians 1:18b-19
213 Romans 8:28

Jezebel had succeeded in turning Israel into Baal worshippers; their destruction as a nation must have seemed certain. Elijah, the prophet, no doubt saw the collision course they were on.

I wonder, what was Elijah ultimately afraid of?

Maybe, like me, he wondered if at the end of the day God really does win? Maybe, like Jezebel, evil wins because we can't seem to hold our end of the bargain, we can't keep the faith? Is God's covenant promise dependent on our faithfulness, our morality? If so, I am doomed. And as I ask this question, I can feel it tap right into the root of that same old ancient lie whispered in the Garden of Eden—*God's not really good.*

Are we back to this again? I thought this had been settled.

What do I still need to process God?

"I invited you to dance. It takes time to learn the moves and lots of repetition to become confident in moving this way. Trust me that as you spiral backwards, you will spring forward."

The dance! Yes, a dance is not one-sided, it's reciprocal. One moves, the other moves. It is an intimate connection that requires trust; it is not one giving command and the other trying to follow; nor is it one doing all the work and the other sitting down. Traditionally in ballroom dancing the male leads, I have heard that if the leader knows how to dance, he can enable a female who doesn't know how to dance to glide across the floor.

"...as a bridegroom rejoices over his bride, so will your God rejoice over you."[214]

God is the bridegroom; I am the bride. Hence, he is the male in this relationship. In this dance He is gently leading me to move in ways I have never done before and into places I have never considered.

I see the Lord before me, offering me his hand to lead me in this present dance. I take his hand, we step backwards, and I remember the day overt evil entered my world, when my friend was kidnapped and killed. Even now, I can hear the enemy of my soul's whisper: *God's impotent! He is no more than a myth!*

---

214 Isaiah 62:5b

Suddenly the dance is on, picking up speed and I feel the need to breathe in deep, then exhale… and again.

I can feel the contractions of my soul picking up in intensity trying to find words for what has grown within me since Dad's death.

The evening before Sept 11, 2001, when Dad resigned from the church, I watched a fatigue creep over him. The emotional responsibility of caring for the congregation and wrestling with his board left him weary. In a year we would discover that the arteries to his heart were 99% blocked and that open-heart surgery would be imminent.

We were blessed with ten more years with Dad after this, but though damage was postponed, in truth, it was already done.

In August of 2011, a mass was discovered growing inside Dad's chest cavity. It was 7.6 pounds, the same weight as my second baby! They removed it with hopes that they had gotten it all. Six months later, when the call came that Dad's cancer was back with a fury, we were told that it was a rather rare form of cancer, with only 800 cases worldwide and that they could not determine the cause of it. The only link to such kinds of cancer seemed to be TRAUMA. It was very likely that Dad's original cancer mass began as a reaction to the open-heart surgery which seemed to be caused by his emotional fatigue and weariness of carrying the church. In the end then, it seemed that the insidious evil that had kicked him out of the church ultimately succeeded in killing him.

Instead of the vindication that I hoped to see for Dad, a restoration back into ministry with a greater sense of power and authority, I saw Dad lose his ministry, most of the elderly care business that he ran after his pastorate and then die.

Deliverance??? Really, God???

Evil seemed to win, just as when my friend was found dead. And I can hear it gloating now as I did then: "God's indifferent! God's impotent! God's dead!"

Moreover, as a witness to this religious spirit, was this not the same insidious spirit that wielded its power against Jesus and seemingly succeeded? I see the seething eyes again that I met when I stepped down off the stage from speaking and a panic rises within me.

"Our struggle is not against flesh and blood, but against the rulers, against the authorities, against the powers of this dark world and against the spiritual forces of evil in the heavenly realms."[215]

It would seem that the same spirit that killed Christ would now try to kill me. And suddenly I know that it was not a woman I was afraid of, but rather an entity that was present in that moment.

What I fear is how this evil, religious-looking spirit can turn people against people, friend against friend, family member against family member. This has been my oppressor my whole life. The religious spirit has been my bully. And it has tried to bully the world in the name of Crusades, denominations, ISIS or any other place where religion has brought death.

I am ashamed of the deep question in my heart. But what if this thing cannot be stopped? Increasing circumstantial evidence would suggest that it is more powerful than the God I know. No wonder I didn't rebuke that oppressive blackness. And suddenly I understand why I want to leave this area. It feels like I have come to my bully's hometown. Of course, such evil has been found the world over. But in a small town, there is nowhere to hide. When a religious spirit mixes with small-town thinking it creates a molotov cocktail; its ignition can dismember anyone standing in its path. Is this why I am walking on eggshells, constantly looking over my shoulder and tiptoeing around hoping I won't be seen?

Sometimes it's hard to tell the difference between what is real and what is counterfeit. When everyone around you seems to be living according to the rules of the culture in the name of God, it can be difficult to discern truth from lies. Furthermore, it can be scary to stand up for the truth, often it means we stand alone. But then again, maybe it is easier to stand alone than it is to dance before the crowd? I think of all the Christians that tolerated, accepted and blessed slavery in the United States. I contrast that with the blind man of Jesus' day who knew he had encountered the Messiah when he could see. He and others were thrown out of their synagogues for daring to believe that God existed beyond the parameters they had been given.

---

215 Ephesians 6:12

A valued friend here in Southland explained how he had gone to a 'revival' prayer meeting the year before we arrived. As they began to pray, he found himself beginning to cry, weep, then wail.

My friend was kicked out of the meeting for 'inappropriate' behaviour.

And I remembered the verse given to me that first year in my kitchen when the Lord and his angels visited.

"Weep and grieve until the spirit is poured out from on high."[216]

So now what?

Am I stuck? When is the promised Spirit to be poured out?

How can I serve God here when I am not sure He can defeat the bully that I face daily?

I hear the voice of God in a verse: *"For the Son of Man did not come to be served, but to serve, and to give his life as a ransom for many."*[217]

Pardon me? What was that, God?

"Hang on, Sarah. It is true, the religious spirit threatened me via the religious rulers of the day. They seemed to win. But the truth is that I came to give my life. I laid down my own life. They did not, could not take my life. Remember: ***"The enemy comes to kill, steal and destroy, but I have come to give you life abundantly."***[218]

I am suddenly aware of how just the slightest twist of the truth can bind me.

Once again, I feel a swift chiropractor-like jolt to my thoughts, bringing them back into alignment. It's true: Jesus gave up his own life. Satan, via the religious leaders of the day, could not have touched him, had they not been permitted to do so. Was this not also true of Job?

I hear it again: Jesus gave up His own life. The religious spirit manifesting through the High Priest Caiaphas did not get to kill him.

And what I understand is that evil may assert itself as triumphant, but it does not get the last word.

---

216 Isaiah 32:15 (MSG)
217 Mark 10:45
218 John 10:10

I am left to sit with that—to let it penetrate.

Eventually my thoughts go back to Elijah, in his pain, flailing emotionally in the desert and the Angel of the Lord coming to tend to him. God feeds, nurtures and soothes Elijah in this place, just as he has been doing with me.

It is interesting to note that the cross-reference story to Elijah being tended to by the Lord is of a young servant girl named Hagar. Centuries before, she too had an encounter with the living God in this place of Beersheba. *"She gave this name to the Lord who spoke to her: 'You are the God who sees me, for I have now seen the one who sees me."*[219]

Is this the same place that I am being brought to? In the deepest place of our hearts, do we not long for God to see us?

I feel the eyes of God on me and consider Elijah and the servant girl. The first was a mighty and powerful agent of God; the latter, a lost nobody; at any given moment, both are true of me. Have I not been discovering that this faith walk is not just about what I have done; good or bad, or what anyone else has done for that matter; but that seeing God truly for who He is is to accept an invitation to dance? To allow Him to gently lead us into the desert where He can speak tenderly to us, revealing His true nature?

As Elijah, the mighty miracle worker, lies under the broom tree, God's actions seem to be reminding him: *"Remember, your worth is not in what you are doing for me, but in whom you have your being."*

I saw Jesus lay me across the Father's lap to be revived. I now hear the same words directed to me: *"Remember, your worth is not in what you are doing for me, but in whom you have your being."* I look again and now see that I have been inflated enough to make the next leg of the journey.

Am I willing to go the distance?

---

219 Genesis 16:13

promise

an invitation to see beyond the temporal

"The cave you fear to enter holds the treasure you seek."

-Joseph Campbell

Elijah goes the distance. He walks forty days and nights across the desert.

What's with the forty days and nights theme in the Bible? Noah was in the storm on the ark for forty days and nights, Moses was on Mt. Sinai forty days and nights, even Jesus himself was in the desert forty days and nights. Ironically, I note that I was forty years old when this upside-down journey began.

The commentary refers to the number forty as representing a time of testing, yet strangely, being with God in that testing. I wonder if it's another way to view the darkness of the inside of the cube—of being centred deep within the heart of God himself?

Elijah arrives at Mt. Horeb, otherwise known as Mt. Sinai.

I note from yet another commentary that there are two meanings for Horeb:

'Desolation after a Great Battle'

and 'A Place to Fend off an Attack.'[220]

The meanings are not lost on me. It feels like we have been through a massive battle that ended in desolation after ten years with Dad's death. Living in Southland seems to have set me up for feeling vulnerable to ongoing attacks. Have I been brought to this moment to fend off an attack?

The first thing I see Elijah do is crawl into a cave and spend the night. He rests.

I think back to my request when Dad was dying, "Now show me your glory!" I didn't realize then that what I was really asking was: How can any good come from this?

---

220 Wikja.org, 'Horeb,' accessed October 14, 2019, https://religion.wikia.org/wiki/Mount_Horeb

God's response was a verse to hold onto:

"The Lord said, I will cause all my goodness to pass in front of you and I will proclaim my name, the Lord, in your presence. There is a place near me where you may stand on a rock. When my glory passes by, I will put you in a cleft in the rock and cover you with my hand until I have passed by. Then I will remove my hand and you will see my back: but my face must not be seen."[221]

And all I can think is, is this not where I have been? I have been resting; trusting that when I find myself, between a rock and a hard place, in the dark with God's hand clearly covering it all, then it is a time to rest in the fact that when I am weak and lost, God is strong and knows exactly where I am.

It has been a long dark night in the cave of my soul, and I have been trusting that God will send me a signal when it is over.

I arrive in Central Otago to an old tuberculosis sanatorium that has been renovated as a retreat centre called En Hakkore. Here all distractions have been removed and I am alone in a wide-open space allowing me to admit how tired I am. I retire into my room for a fitful and cold night's sleep.

As I wake, I am overwhelmed with a strange form of grief that at first I can't identify. I am acutely aware that I am all alone in a strange place. I am also alert to some invisible fingerprints in the room—*Death* has been here before.

I hear the name 'Elizabeth' running through my mind. My middle name, also my daughter's name, seems to be only used in its entirety when someone is in trouble. I hear it again and am reminded of its meaning: *'Elizabeth: Promise of God.'*

My thoughts turn to the woman from whom I draw my middle name and for whom my daughter was named, my father's mother. I never knew my grandmother Elizabeth; neither did my father for that matter, not really.

Waking in this strange place, to its aged and dated hospital-green walls, I feel slightly panicked. I wonder about my father's mother, Elizabeth.

---

221 Exodus 33:19-22

I have only known facts about her until now, and not many. Just 28 years old, she died with tuberculosis leaving behind two small boys and a baby. But as I lay in this bed, trying to stay warm, the residue of Death's fingerprints in this room makes fear palpable. Was she afraid?

I imagine a young woman postpartum who should be voluptuous with milk-swollen breasts, instead frail with consumption. My memory recalls having had to nurse one of my babies once while I had a fever. Every time the baby would suckle, pain seared through me. And yet it was worth it, holding that beautiful little angel in my arms. But Elizabeth, fevered, breasts leaking and no baby in her arms—how did she not go mad? I feel a mind-losing grief. I was told that she was a woman of faith. What kind of prayers did she pray?

No sooner do I ask that I hear an echo of my own, feeling a new connection with my grandmother; *Are you really out there, God? Who are you, God? Do you know what you are doing, God? If you can, why don't you? Do you have my kids?*

I remember my father telling me once of his only real memory of his mother, a bit vague but treasured. He remembered looking out the back window of a car up to a second-story window of the sanatorium where his mother was waving goodbye to him as the car drove slowly away.

Maybe the blockage or trauma in Dad's heart started decades before? Maybe the enemy is not that creative. Maybe he just knows how to press on our soft spots. He knows how and where to add a little insult to injury, in hopes of clogging an artery, or multiplying malignant cells.

"Who then can rescue me from this body of death?"[222]

I know that I am supposed to answer 'God.' Technically my head gets that that is the answer according to scripture. But I am not comfortable with it, or maybe, not satisfied is the real term. The pat answer without deeper understanding is like cotton candy in the mouth.

Elizabeth: Promise…

What promise???

---

222 Romans 7:24b

I turn to my New Testament in search of the original Elizabeth in the Bible, John the Baptist's mother. Maybe it will grant me some understanding…

"In the time of Herod king of Judea there was priest named Zechariah, who belonged to the priestly division of Abijah; his wife Elizabeth was also a descendent of Aaron. Both of them were upright in the sight of God, observing all the Lord's commandments and regulations blamelessly. But they had no children, because Elizabeth was barren; and they were both well along in years."[223]

I already know that Elizabeth means *promise*, but I wonder why it notes that she is a descendent of Aaron. That is, until my morning One Year Bible reading once again obliges:

"Aaron was set apart, he and his descendants forever, to consecrate the most holy things, to offer sacrifices before the Lord, to minister before him and to pronounce blessings in his name forever."[224]

Did Elizabeth understand that she was part of this legacy?

Clearly the scripture comments on her being blameless, righteous, before it tells us that she is barren. At first I wonder how old Elizabeth might be? What I do know is that she is not a young wife; if her heart's desire was for children, would not each passing day be a nail in the coffin of hope? I then wonder why the scripture comments on their righteousness as a couple. It seems very intentional to clear their name in some way. I find the cross-reference verses and read on for a bit in the book of Deuteronomy when I discover this promise from the Jewish Torah:

"If you pay attention to these laws and are careful to follow them, then the Lord your God will keep his Covenant of love with you, as he swore to your forefathers. He will love you and bless you and increase your numbers. He will bless the fruit of your womb, the crops of your land…"[225]

There is a conditional, almost transactional promise that if one honours God, He will then honour them. The scripture seems full of statements

223 Luke 1:5-7
224 1 Chronicles 23:13
225 Deuteronomy 7:12-13

like this. For a moment, I begin to falter; I know this way. I have treated my relationship with God in the past as a contract to be observed; if I do my part, then He will do His; If I am faithful to him, then He will bless me. But the invitation to dance has made me let go of trying to keep control by observing certain measures. I can feel myself waiver in my new understanding…have I got that wrong?

Even more disturbing is that I note that Elizabeth is doing her part, why isn't God doing His? Does God not keep his promises???

I wonder about the questions Elizabeth must have carried within her. Had she not tried to keep the covenant requirements? Did she feel like perhaps something in her was deeply unworthy? Did she feel like God had rejected her? Or on the flip side, did she ever doubt God's goodness? Did the enemy of her soul ever whisper to her like he did to me, *God is indifferent, impotent or dead*? The shame and disgrace she must have carried among her people who believed that this transactional salvation was the way of God, mixed with her own disappointment with each passing month, must have been nearly unbearable. But even more so, how could she pronounce the blessings of God to another, when she herself had yet to encounter God in this way personally? Was she just going through the motions? Or was she in a place of deep trust? The scriptures don't tell.

As a result of this journey through Antipodes and reading the story of Elijah with fresh eyes, I wonder much more about the human struggle these characters had in order to believe and see God move on their behalf. In the past, I would have thought of Elizabeth as some transcendent character who maintained an unwavering steadfast spirit in the face of her own trial. Sometimes the foreknowledge I have of the outcome of a Bible story can negate the human side of the characters; 'Look what God did!' But they were human, waiting for answers just like me, doing their best to think that somehow in the midst of life's impossibilities, God could still be good.

I can't think of one Bible story where God doesn't ultimately win, where love doesn't win. And yet, it wouldn't seem God won in Dad's situation—no life with his mama, no restoration to the lies spoken over his reputation, no financial restoration, no healing. I think of different Bible characters and once again land back on Job. I am sure that in the thick of things Job didn't think God was going to win. Job lost everything, even his children died and yet at the end of the story, God still wins and blesses Job. Clearly then, God can still work His good even in death and he can still proclaim his name over us while we are between a rock and a hard place in the dark.

I am curious about Zechariah, Elizabeth's husband's name. The baby name book that helped us name four of our own children still sits on the shelf; I reach for it and discover that Zechariah means *The Lord Remembers*.[226]

So, I summarize that in the time of Herod, a wannabe king of the Jews, the Lord sets the stage to reveal himself through two righteous people whose names together mean *The Lord Remembers His Promise*. Ironically, they have both yet to know personally God's favour as promised. It's the perfect opening for a play and although I have heard this story often at Christmas, I have never seen it like this before; it makes me keen to reread what follows.

Zechariah, chosen by lot, is to go into the temple of the Lord to burn incense, while worshippers wait outside and pray. During his time in the temple, Zechariah has an encounter with an angel who tells him that he and his wife will have a baby and they are to name him John. The angel announces:

He will be a joy and a delight to you, and many will rejoice because of his birth, for he will be great in the sight of the Lord…many he will bring back to the Lord their God. And he will go on before the Lord, in the spirit and power of Elijah, to turn the hearts of the fathers to their children and the disobedient to the wisdom of the righteous –to make ready a people prepared for their God."[227]

I am stunned. The promise is linked to Elijah in the Old Testament, the very prophet I have been dissecting. What am I to see? I turn to Malachi and understand that the last few verses of the Old Testament before four hundred years of silence is the promise of the return of Elijah.

Elijah? Four hundred years of silence!?

---

226 Bruce Lansky. *The Best Baby Name Book in the Whole Wide World.* (New York, Simon and Schuster, 1984), 137
227 Luke 1:14-17

"For a long time, I have kept silent, I have been quiet and held myself back. But now, like a woman in childbirth, I cry out, I gasp and pant."[228]

Four hundred years is a long pregnancy, a long time to let cells divide, multiply and grow undercover. The fullness of time in pregnancy is when the creation is ready to be born; something in the angel's announcement to *Zechariah, the Lord Remembers*, is to signify that John will be arriving and will help the earth prepare for the birth of the long-awaited promise of the Messiah.

John's name means *God is Gracious.*[229]

The dictionary says that *Gracious* means: *pleasantly kind, benevolent and courteous; indulgent or beneficent in a pleasantly condescending way, especially to inferiors; and merciful or compassionate*[230]

Certainly, God shows his mercy and compassion to this couple. Elizabeth who has been waiting to see God's promise fulfilled to her personally as well as that of her people, undoubtedly laughs with great joy as baby John is laid in her arms.

Finally, she beholds the promise.

Embracing her newborn son, there is no question that Elizabeth now understands first-hand the compassionate God that can redeem a barren woman. Does hope rise in her on behalf of her people? Does she realise that she is a walking illustration of God's grace and what he will do for not just her, but her people? Does she realise that God's gracious manner will extend beyond just her people and will move Him to rescue all those who are barren, without life, roaming through the desert of their souls?

The message of John's life was this:

"A voice of one calling in the desert, 'Prepare the way for the Lord', Make straight paths for him. Every valley shall be filled in. Every mountain and hill made low. The crooked roads shall become

---

228   Isaiah 42:14
229   Lansky. *The Best Baby Name Book,* 111
230   Dictionary.com, 'Gracious,' accessed October 12, 2019, https://www.dictionary.com/browse/gracious?s=t

straight, the rough ways smooth. And all mankind will see God's salvation."[231]

Certainly, the longest road I have ever travelled is from my head to my heart. Even as I have been traveling through Antipodes, the Holy Spirit has graciously gone before me, filling in the potholes on this road, removing the obstacles that keep me from moving forward and smoothing out my rough edges.

Staring at the green walls I hear it again: *Elizabeth –Promise of God.*

I understand that the Bible character received her promise in the fullness of time, both personally and for her people. Her darkness gave way for God's light to display the brightness of his redemption plan. And in hindsight, God's delay seemed to only highlight His blessing, to make Himself more known, to reveal His glory. Is that meant to be true for me as well? Certainly, God has been bringing all kinds of light into my darkness.

I wait. Is there something else to be seen in relation to my grandmother Elizabeth? To me?

Randomly I find myself thinking about time; certainly it is not what it seems. Moving through life, I am generally bound to move from point A to point B before I can reach point C; I was born before I turned three, before I turned ten years old. Yet when I read Elizabeth's story in the Bible and think about the moment that her empty arms were filled with a beautiful baby boy, I think of a moment that defies time as I know it. A baby isn't generally born past childbearing years, but with God all things are possible. John's birth was a moment in 'the set time;' and with this I remember that God has his own time and a greater clock outside of time as I know it. God is not limited to earth's time.

BAM!

And with this thought comes an understanding about my father's death, suddenly everything seems to come full circle in my mind. With an absolute clarity I can see that 'time' as I experience it is not real, or at least not the same in all spheres. God's greater time clock outside of earth could be called 'the fullness of time;' the apostle Paul writes

---

231 Luke 3:4-6

189

about it in Galatians: ***"But when the fulness of time was come, God sent forth his Son, made of a woman…"[232]***

The Presence now nudges me: What did you witness *in the fulness of time* concerning your father?

I start to reel: Somehow God in his graciousness let me see a glimpse of my father and his mother's reunion; a glimpse of the restoration of what was stolen 65 years before! I remember the vision I had of my father's mother reminding the Lord of their agreement, of their promise. I remember my father pointing and calling to his 'Ma!' hours before his death. I was privileged to witness a glimpse of their story. Time could not keep the promise of being together again from being fulfilled. And I grasp that what is promised as I walk earth's timeline will be completed, whether I can see it from where I am standing in time or not.

"For no matter how many promises God has made, they are 'Yes' in Christ."[233]

Dad made a video of his last sermon for his funeral. He said something at the end that was rather shocking:

"I'm not going to miss you. Not really. Why? Cause I'm going to see you soon. Maybe in an hour or so?"

That made people shift in their seats rather uncomfortably before he went on:

"See, heaven's time is different. God said a day is like 1000 years and 1000 years a day. Imagine then what 10-20 years might be in that scope of things. -Maybe 15 minutes, if that? I'll be waiting for you. I love you…and I'll see you soon!"

Sitting in this green room, I am stunned. I was witness to this very thing.

His mother Elizabeth, *Promise of God* was waiting. God's promises were waiting. All those years of aching, of heartache and abandonment, were healed in an instant on his deathbed. He called her name, pointed to her and then laid back peacefully. The great questions and longings of his heart finally healed.

---

232 Galatians 4:4
233 2 Corinthians 1:20

The ultimate truth then is that God's promises are never late, never forgotten! They are always fulfilled and always on time in the fullness of time!

I go for a walk and end up on a visit with the woman who had the vision for starting this retreat centre. We talk, share our stories. I say the last four years have been interesting. I tell her some things, but not about Elijah. Before I leave, she says she wants to read me something. She grabs her Bible and proceeds to read me the same story I have been mulling about, Elijah. When she is finished, she looks up, makes sure I am listening and then says: "It's time to come out of the cave, dear."

– I have been 'signalled.'

And I think I am ready, awake.

conversation

an invitation to honest dialogue

" Set me free from evil passions and heal my heart of all inordinate affections;
that being inwardly cured and thoroughly cleansed,
I may be fit to love, courageous to suffer, steady to persevere. "

-Thomas a Kempis

I return to my room and re-read the story in 1 Kings 19.

"And the word of the Lord came to him: "What are you doing here Elijah?"²³⁴

God initiates the conversation. And I know He is about to do the same with me.

I watch the strange prayer that unfolds.

Elijah admits that he feels like his work has not been worth anything, that he lacks confidence that God's kingdom will advance and that he would like to withdraw from the present arena of conflict.

Hmm. Sounds familiar.

He replied, "I have been very zealous for the Lord God almighty. The Israelites have rejected your covenant, broken down your altars, and put your prophets to death with the sword. I am the only one left, and now they are trying to kill me too. "²³⁵

And I can hear my own heart echoing: "I am working my heart out here for you, God. And the people are strange, it's always cold and it always smells of coal. I am all alone here without any family or support. I'm dying."

I note the scriptures and God's question just seems to sit there, with Elijah's response. God doesn't rebuke Elijah, nor does he answer him. What is going on?

---

234 1 Kings 19:9b
235 1 Kings 19:10

I see my own spoken words floating in the air before me. God's just looking at them. I look at them and see that they are distorted, warbling. I hear the emphasis on 'always', 'all' and can hear myself say, *"Okay, Okay, it's not 'always' cold, it doesn't 'always' smell of coal, not 'all' the people are strange and some of the most supportive people live here and have been very kind and giving to us."*

I note Elijah's words. They are distorted too. Not everyone had broken the covenant, not all the prophets had been murdered, not all the altars were destroyed, and he was not the only one left. *It may have felt that way,* but it was not the truth.

The Lord said, "Go-out and stand on the mountain in the presence of the Lord, for the Lord is about to pass by."[236]

The cross-reference verse is once again to Moses.

"Then the Lord came down in the cloud and stood there with him and proclaimed his name, the Lord. And he passed in front of Moses, proclaiming, "The Lord, the lord, the compassionate and gracious God, slow to anger, abounding in love and faithfulness, maintaining love to thousands, and forgiving wickedness, rebellion and sin. Yet he does not leave the guilty unpunished."[237]

Have I not been discovering what it looks like for God to proclaim His name before me?

I switch back to Elijah's story.

I note the mighty acts of God to follow; powerful winds that shattered the rocks, an earthquake and then a fire. But God was not in any of them.

A gentle whisper was spoken, and Elijah knew it was the voice of God.

God then asks him the same question: *"What are you doing here Elijah?"[238]*

Twice, God asks Elijah the same question, always a signal to pay attention.

I focus.

---

236 1 Kings 19:11
237 Exodus 34:5-7
238 1 Kings 19:13b

Suddenly I see the Lion of Judah turn towards me and roar.

The roar seems to rattle the apathetic weary places of my heart. "Awake!"

Then I hear the still small voice, *"Look again, Sarah. Reach deeper."*

Something deep within groans. Something else needs to be spoken.

It's true, there is another level to go.

So, I reach deeper…

"Alright God, I feel as if I have been working my heart out for you!"

"Yes."

"But the church Dad was a pastor at never fully reconciled with him, Dad lost the business, you didn't heal him, the evil spirit succeeded in killing him and now it's trying to kill me."

"Good. That's the feeling. What's the truth?"

What? The truth?

"Do you remember how many came to his funeral from far and wide? Do you remember the binder full of letters to him expressing their gratefulness for his ministry to them?"

"Yes."

"Sarah, I am faithful to people, not necessarily to institutions. None of your father's sacrifice, love or service was lost in heaven's economy."

"Oh."

I try to digest this.

"Next item of business: did the whole business belly up?"

"No. It should have. It just about did."

"I salvaged it. And I have made it what it needs to be for your sister to take it where it needs to be."

I feel as if God is cleaning a very dirty pair of eyeglasses that I am wearing.

"Next: Did the 'religious' spirit succeed in killing him? In the end, did it get to claim him?

"N....o?"

"Why?"

"I saw you come for him. At 4:22, you came and took him home."

"Will I let it kill you?"

"No. You promised that when it was my time to go home that you would come for me."

"What are you believing, Sarah?"

"Lies."

"Where do they come from?"

The father of lies?

"Yes...crafted by the enemy of your soul."

"Sarah, Sarah, Satan has asked permission to sift you like wheat, but I have prayed for you and when you have turned back, strengthen your brothers and sisters."[239]

"I remember you said that to me before we came to New Zealand."

"Yes."

"Does that mean the time of testing, or hardship is over?"

"What did your father use to say about faith steps?"

"That they just keep getting bigger and bigger. Every lesson pre-learned builds the strength and faith to leap a little further or higher the next time."

"Are you afraid of that?"

"Yes."

"What do you fear?"

---

239 Luke 22:3

"That I will have to stand alone or that I will fail to stand alone."

"Never will I leave you or forsake you!"

"What if I fail you?"

"Then you will be in good company. No human ever gets it fully right. Look at Elijah, see how I gave him instructions and he actually failed to do the first two. He only went and named his successor."

"Wow. But you still used him?"

"Of course. This is a relationship, not a contract. Like Elijah, you are not done. I still have more purposes for you ahead. You are not alone, and I will bring you help. I want to move you into a fuller purpose of who I am and how I move. Remember, I don't need you to defend me, I just need you to love me. Life will flow out of 'us.'"

I go back and look at the instructions that God gave to Elijah.

GOD said, "Go back the way you came through the desert to Damascus. When you get there anoint Hazael; make him king... Then anoint Jehu; make him king over Israel. Finally, anoint Elisha...to succeed you as prophet...Meanwhile, I'm preserving for myself seven thousand souls: the knees that haven't bowed to the god Baal, the mouths that haven't kissed his image."[240]

Obviously, I am not being called to anoint any kings.

Yet one command grips my soul: *"Go back the way you came!"*

---

240 1 Kings 19:15-18

return

an invitation to trust God with our children

"The new voyage of discovery consists not in seeking new landscapes, but in having new eyes."

-Marcel Proust

"Go back the way you came!"

Go back?

"Yes!"

Go back forty days and nights across the desert?

"Yes, you need time with just me, to let things solidify in you.

The road to Horeb, the place to heal after a great desolation, was long and arduous, in part due to the deep questions of your heart that gave fear access. Crossing the province of poverty has taught you your own need and that there is a Hope beyond hope. Hunger territory has dared you to dance with Love, the place of Weeping has opened avenues to My joy and facing this territory of Oppression is making you wrestle for true and authentic Peace.

In deep levels you are understanding that you are my daughter. You are my girl, whom I have chosen, marked with my love and with whom I am well pleased."

My heart dares to receive God's words of pleasure in me, but fear knocks quietly at the door. I note that right after God announces His pleasure in Jesus, He hands Jesus over to Satan in the desert.

Lord? Why? Why did you do that?

"Remember how the LORD your God led you all the way in the wilderness these forty years, to humble and test you in order to know what was in your heart, whether or not you would keep his commands. He humbled you, causing you to hunger and then feeding you with manna, which neither you nor your ancestors had known, to teach

you that man does not live on bread alone but on every word that comes from the mouth of the LORD. Your clothes did not wear out and your feet did not swell during these forty years. Know then in your heart that as a man disciplines his son, so the LORD your God disciplines you.[241]

As I hear these words, I see a garden, a beautiful rich garden full of fruit, veggies and flowers. It is masterful. Suddenly it is stripped back to just dirt. The gardener is testing the soil, tilling and fertilizing it. And I understand that my heart is the garden. My desire is to be the first image. And the invitation is then to trust the gardener to know how to prepare my garden.

On one level I thought I understood God's deep pleasure in me upon my arrival in New Zealand. But as the tidal waves came, old deep-seated lies and fears took their opportunity to weed their way up.

I hear this continual whisper: *"I know how to test your heart, to make you ready, to establish true authority within you. Will you trust me to satisfy your hunger? Will you trust my means of getting you to the goal? Will you trust me to protect you? Do you trust that 'what has happened to you will work out for your deliverance?"*

Trust? *"Firm belief in the honesty, reliability of some person or thing."*

Even now, I still find myself stumbling over the word 'deliverance.' It sounds so victorious. I am certain that God can and will work all things together for good, but 'deliverance' conjures up images of an operation rescue mission for me. I did not see God work in this way. There was no angel swat team descending into my father's bedroom, rescuing him from the hideous beast of cancer.

I find myself muttering to the Lord, "You didn't deliver Dad from death, nor did you deliver the Apostle Paul from prison. As I move forward in my life, what guarantee do I have that you will deliver me?"

I feel set up, no sooner have I asked this question, an answer is provided in an unexpected way. I take a break, go for a ride and end up listening to a talk on the book of Philippians by Shane Willard.

---

241 Deuteronomy 8:2-5

Willard mentions Paul's attitude, the very one that reminded me of Dad's posture in dying; *"I will continue to rejoice, for I know that through your prayers and the help given by the Spirit of Jesus Christ, what has happened to me will turn out for my deliverance."* [242]

Willard then begins to unpack how the Apostle Paul could have such confidence in making this statement. One particular and powerful sentence out of Shane's mouth has me pulling the car over to the side of the road to absorb what he says:

"The ancient Jewish tradition of wisdom literature says that 'my deliverance' does not mean the ceasing of suffering, it means that when one gets through a situation, they will be able to stand before God with clean hands, a pure heart and a sweet taste in the mouth." [243]

Suddenly I realise that if this is the definition, I indeed saw God deliver my father.

I am floored!

Tears of recognition begin to fall down my face as I remember an interaction with my father during one of the last weeks of his life. One afternoon we had an interesting conversation as he was stirring from a nap.

"Hi ya Daddy, how are you doing?"

He tried to moisten his lips before he spoke, "I think this is the last day."

Putting a glass of water up to his lips for a sip, I ask, "The last day of what, Dad?"

He said softly, "Climbing the mountain…"

I tried to clarify the whisper of an answer, "The mountain?"

"Yeah"—

"What kind of mountain, Dad?"

"The mountain of purification."

"And then you will die?" I asked, anxiety creeping up behind me.

---

242 Philippians 1:16
243 Shane Willard, *Philippians Part 1, My Deliverance*, Shane Willard Ministries, 2018

"Oh, I don't know about that…"

As we talked, it became apparent that there was deep work going on inside of Dad. In his dying process, the Lord was metaphorically washing Dad's hands, purifying his heart and making any bitter taste in Dad's mouth sweet. By the definition of the Jewish tradition of ancient wisdom literature, God was indeed delivering my father. Maybe not in the way I had hoped, an operational rescue mission, but in truth, like a midwife gently preparing a mother to birth her child. I was privileged to catch a glimpse of God preparing my father to meet him.

This revelation spreads between my memories, gluing together fragmented pieces, solidifying that I did in truth see God deliver my father. How many times did my mother, sister and I say that there was something in Dad's dying process that felt reminiscent of pregnancy and labour? Did I not ask, "What will I name that which is being born in my father's dying?"

Memory links to my first Sunday at church after Dad died. Friends surrounded me with love and prayers. One lady said, "Just remember these words, Sarah; 'Hope beyond hope!' God will give you Hope beyond hope." Suddenly, I realise that this whole book of questions has been my own mountain of purification to climb, a means of giving me Hope beyond hope. Have not all my doubts and questions been leading me on a search for light, allowing God to wash my hands, purify my heart and make the bitter taste in my mouth sweet? I have been asking, will God deliver me? Apparently, by this definition, He is already in the process of doing so.

I hear the question I wrote many pages and now years ago echo in my ears, "If hope is not in an outcome, but in a BEING, what do we do when we are not sure we can trust that Being?"

I came to Antipodes thinking I knew how to trust. Maybe I knew how to for myself, but I confess that when I began to see my whole family begin to spiral downwards, when I began to see my children flailing in the midst of it all, trust was demanded at a whole new level. Now I understand my initial vision in the kitchen all those years ago. When the Lord and His angels had appeared, I understood in theory that my roots would have to push deeper, anchoring themselves under the rock. And how I have been learning to do that!

O God, forgive me for my lack of trust.

"He led you through the vast and dreadful wilderness, that thirsty and waterless land, with its venomous snakes and scorpions. He brought you water out of hard rock. He gave you manna to eat in the wilderness, something your ancestors had never known, to humble and test you so that in the end it might go well with you. You may say to yourself, "My power and the strength of my hands have produced this wealth for me." But remember the LORD your God, for it is he who gives you the ability to produce wealth, and so confirms his covenant, which he swore to your ancestors, as it is today."[244]

And with tears, I am deeply humbled. I have been tested, tried. And where I have lacked faith, trust, hope, love, joy and peace, God has steadily given me His water, His manna...

Any illusion of Sarah Almighty walking the streets is gone.

The world around me says, "Go on! Make it happen! Chase those dreams!"

But I say, "Here I am, Lord, with all my hopes and dreams. They are yours. You are the only one I trust. I will believe and wait for your strength, direction, energy and provision."

"They that wait upon the Lord, shall renew their strength..."[245]

Wait: to stay in a place or remain inactive until something expected takes place, to be ready, to remain temporarily undone, to be, remain or delay expectation of...

For some reason I keep thinking of Jesus' disciples that got stuck out all night in the boat trying to catch fish. It was when they were ready to give up, admit that they couldn't catch anything in all their trained fishermen ways, that Jesus told them to cast their nets on the other side; all at once there was an influx of fish. This is a new level of trust. Jesus is not asking to use all my gifts, talents etc; He already has access to those. What He is asking for surprises me; He wants to use my nothingness. Just maybe, it is harder to step out or into God's bidding when we feel we have nothing.

I wonder, did Elijah feel stripped to nothing after his desert encounter?

244 Deuteronomy 8:15-18
245 Isaiah 40:31 (KJV)

The Bible doesn't talk about his return trip. I wonder, was God deepening Elijah's trust in Him as they walked back across the desert? And why was it important for Elijah to go back through Beersheba, to the Oath-Well, again? What did God want to solidify there in Elijah? Did Elijah even go back? The scriptures don't tell.

We do know that Elijah would have to return to work, to the place of threat. He would have to deal once again with the wayward nation that he was called to lead. What did God need him to know, see and understand? Would something be found at the Oath-Well that might anchor trust?

What does God want me to know, see and understand? Is there something in this that will anchor my trust?

I return to re-examine the oath, the promise. Nothing jumps out at me in 1 Kings 19. I call my mother, tell her all about what I have discovered from Elizabeth. I further explain that Elijah had to go back the way he came, which meant he would have had to have had a pit stop in Beersheba, 'the well of promise' and that I wondered if there was something more to understand about promises: "Mom, do you think that there could be something in my 'traveling back' that might be linked to a promise that Dad was also holding on to?"

Mom can't think of anything except, "Maybe check the original promise or oath made in the Bible." So, I return to the book of Genesis, when Isaac returns to his father's home in Beersheba. I review that on the night Isaac had a dream, that God indeed appeared to him and gave him this promise:

"I am the God of Abraham your father, don't fear a thing because I'm with you."[246]

But this time, I see what I missed the first time round.

"I'll bless you and make your children flourish because of Abraham my servant."[247]

Was Dad trusting God for some greater promise regarding his children, grandchildren? The original promise was made to Abraham and God restated His promise to Abraham's son Isaac and his future descendants. And something in my heart leaps, dares to hope—the promise covered

---

246 Genesis 6:24a
247 Genesis 6:25b

the children!

Was this the anchor meant for Elijah's trust as he returned to deal with a rebellious nation?

***

I grasped the idea of an anchor for Elijah but now need it for myself.

My heart is pounding.

Disoriented, I try to breathe. Sweat pours from my brow as I try to remember the surreal dream reality I was in just moments before.

In the dream, I am in a church…

There are three of us sitting in a pew: My father, my brother and then myself. We stand to sing and I am aware that the people are watching us. I can feel the murmurs. The disapproval when my brother reluctantly stands to do what others do. His long, knotted, uncombed hair and untidy appearance raises unseen questions.

I can feel my brother's disdain for this 'house.' The cheesy worship songs, the people like unsuspecting sheep, all unoriginal thinkers; he pokes at their judgemental, back-biting carnivorous ways by throwing a paper wad across the room as we sing.

I want Dad to take control, to say, "Son, this is not an appropriate way to act here. Stop it!" He doesn't. Instead I hear the gasps and murmurs of the people as I watch the paper wad hit the screen with the worship words on them.

I am aware of a rebellious spirit rising in my brother and I try to compensate for it by singing harder. Somehow I must cover him, I believe in him, in who he is; I can't turn my back on him, disown him, because I see the greatness of God in him.

I can't really hear what is going on in the service. What I can pick up is tedious—boring. My brother is right. It feels suddenly like I am in a game; everybody planning their next play. I know in my gut that this isn't how church should be, but I also know that I can't turn my back on it; there is supposed to be something more here, I can see the untapped greatness of God here.

Horror grips me when I realize that Dad isn't doing anything because he isn't there; he's dead and suddenly I understand that we are at his funeral.

The service continues to be laborious. My brother gets up and goes to the side of the church and pulls out his computer. Eventually he turns up the sound and plays his video games unabashedly. I get angry, grab his computer and shut it off; this is our father's funeral for goodness sake!

Caring for my brother, protecting my brother, pleading with my brother is a full-time job and the service is over before I can even process my own heart, my own grief.

My brother leaves, everyone leaves, but for one lady and myself.

She has the question in her eyes—*the* question!

How can a man like my father who loves God deeply and has served him his whole life produce an intolerant, belligerent son who openly rejects, if not profanes, the things of God? The question in and of itself is fair enough. I remember wondering why the sons of great men in the Bible; Aaron, Samuel, David and the likes, did not love God?

But that is not what I react to: It is the accusation beneath the question; the sounds of a snake hissing accuser asking a seemingly innocent question that leaves me feeling condemned already.

"So, what really went on in their home?"

The woman is taller than me.

I do not shrink back. I walk up to her, stand on my tiptoes and fiercely speak the truth.

"He is only 15! He can ask questions! He must ask questions to own this himself. Do not judge him!"

I no sooner speak to this lady, that I am gripped with the sudden realization that my brother is now my son.

Before I am fully awake, I see faces of the children of families I know who have seemingly perfect and God-fearing sons. And suddenly, appearances feel quite important.

The *Shoulds* pounce on my vulnerable state with a myriad of contradicting voices…

"You should have encouraged your son to do more sports. Didn't you realize how important that might be for his development in this season of his life?"

"You should have been harder on him! You have been too lenient, too freedom-oriented!"

"You shouldn't make him go to church! You are a control freak…"

Suddenly, I feel as if I am being cross examined, a myriad of questions attacking and undermining any confidence I have had in my parenting.

O God help me! As I thrust myself up and awake!

My mind is racing. "God, what are you after in me?"

***

Now wide awake, memory plays and I can remember how the bumps and grooves in the concrete front steps of my childhood home felt cold and hard beneath me at four years of age. Then, I turned and looked back into the house as I heard my mother scream my name, "Sarah!" There were flames dancing behind her as she ran at me with the baby. "Take him!"

My baby brother, Michael, was thrust in my arms.

Michael means, 'who is like the Lord.'[248]

A piece of God himself was thrown in my arms and I accepted, believed and loved this little miracle.

I turned and watched my courageous mother pick up a mat by the door and run back into the kitchen and hit the flames with the mat as I soothed my brother. She was able to extinguish the fire but not before the smoke had blackened most of the house. Like the smoke blackening the house, a sort of invisible smoke, unbeknownst to me, laid over my soul that day. I didn't know that I had taken on my brother as my responsibility. I didn't know until I went home to be with Dad

---

248 Lansky. *The Best Baby Namebook*, 118

in his dying. My brother had come to visit and had taken his pain out on me with snarky comments. My mother told me to mend it. And suddenly I broke.

"I have tried to carry my brother ever since you threw him at me in that fire. I have carried him in my heart all these years. But he is a grown man now. I have a husband, four children and my own pain to process in all of this. I can't carry a 36-year-old man on my back. I cannot be responsible for my brother's actions or pain."

Dad was weakening. He waved his arm to have me come closer. He pulled me down to where he lay in a reclined chair. I had to get on my knees to hear what he wanted to say. His voice was but whispers. He gently laid my head against his reclining chest. I began to cry for fear that I was causing my dad greater pain with the burden of this family squabble. I feared I had disappointed him. As the eldest, I was trying to hold everything and everyone together. I couldn't, our world was crumbling.

I paid attention to Dad's whispers. His words were quiet, his manner peaceful and as I quieted, I realized that he was praying for me: "Forgive us, God, where we have put undue expectation on Sarah. We ask that you release her now from burdens that she is not meant to carry. Meet Michael. Tend to him as I know you will, God."

His prayer was washing away the invisible smoke from all those years ago. Peace came.

Shortly after this, my brother came to help my dad. And I wondered, in their sacred moments alone, was Dad reassuring his son as he did me?

Dad's name, Ronald Evans, means *Mighty power* and *Grace*.[249]

My brother shared my father's middle name.

I never saw my father stop believing in his son.

Now, in these last days together, could *Grace* be the link between *Mighty power* and *someone who refused to live their destiny to be like the Lord?*

Is it not *Grace* that links the divine and mighty power to us? I have discovered that this is true for those of us who would aspire but find

---

249 Lansky, *The Best Baby Namebook*, 126

ourselves unable, no matter how hard we try to get it right. But will that grace hunt down and pursue one who has deliberately hardened their heart? Perhaps this is my fear: What if Grace gives up on some?

How far does Grace go?

Elijah had to return to deal with a rebellious nation.

And as mentioned in the previous section, God tells Elijah to do three things as he traces his steps back, but Elijah only does one of them: He anoints his successor, Elisha.

Elijah means *Jehovah is God.*[250] And with all his strength, he has urged the people to turn back and worship the one true God. His fears must have mounted when the stubborn hearts of the people refused to worship God alone. And yet it would seem as if God is saying, *"Elijah, listen! You have to trust me! You can't make the people turn around. The people can't even make themselves do it. But I have a plan! I want you to anoint Elisha meaning 'God saves.' Let me show you a glimpse of my heart."* And for a second, God pulls back his shirt, bares his chest and says, *"My heart is to save! I am always looking to restore!"* Yeshua, Jesus, like Elisha means *God saves.*[251]

"God did not send His son into the world to condemn the world, but to save the world through him."[252]

*Elijah, you can't understand this yet. It will become plain in another time, another season than the one you have been called to, but I have a plan. In fact, it was put into motion before you were born, **before the creation of the world.**[253] And it looks like Elisha -God saves! I will complete what my people cannot."*

Fast forwarding several centuries, I think of how John meaning *God is gracious* was to come like Elijah. In the Old Testament, *Jehovah is God* precedes *God Saves.* In the New Testament, *God is Gracious* precedes *God Saves.* The difference seems ever so slight. Elijah's mission was as his name, to declare Jehovah as the one true God to the Israelites. Although John is coming in the spirit of Elijah to declare the one true

250 Ibid. 98
251 Ibid. 127
252 John 3:17
253 1 Peter 1:20

207

God, his name seems even more specific to the nature of the God He is called to prepare the way for: Jesus. The God who saves is gracious.

Gracious: merciful, forgiving, compassionate, kind, kindly, lenient, clement, pitying, forbearing, humane, mild, soft-hearted, tender-hearted, sympathetic, patient, humanitarian, liberal, easy-going, permissive, tolerant, indulgent, generous, magnanimous, beneficent, benign, benignant, benevolent.[254]

I hear God ask me: *"How far will grace go?"*

What? I was asking you that! I look at him blankly. I simply don't know.

Think Sarah…remember what you witnessed!

As if suddenly zapped, my mind flashes instantly back to an evening of watching my mother pace the floor. It was getting late and Dad wasn't home yet.

"Where's Dad?" I asked.

"He went up to San Francisco to see if he could see your brother."

My brother in those days was hard to find. He was often out on the streets somewhere high on methamphetamine.

We waited for what seemed to be an eternity.

Mom sighed a breath of relief when she heard the garage door lift and the purr of the engine shut off in the wee hours of the morning. I could see that she still hoped that her only son might be in the car.

Her eyes wide, cautious hope rising…just maybe her son would walk through the door.

He didn't.

Mom choked back her disappointment, "Did you find him?"

With a weary sigh, Dad answered, "Eventually."

Dad had driven almost three hours up to the city, drove around the city for hours hoping to spot my brother and when he found him, took him to dinner, before he drove all the way back home.

---

254 Definebasket.com, 'Gracious,' accessed October 12, 2019, http://www.definebasket.com/Z3JhY2lvdXM/

The Presence whispers as I recall this memory ...

And I am reduced to tears when I consider a Grace that not only releases us to choose when we are ready but is willing to **demonstrate his love** *to us even when we are not.*

I look into those deep pools again in Jesus' eyes. This time I can see my own children's lives, journeys being reflected. He sees, He knows and it is His responsibility to draw them close to Himself. Instinctively, I understand that this was the same promise Dad was believing in for his children.

"Your servants' children will have a good place to live and their children will be at home with you."[255]

I yield, I trust. And I can feel my roots burrow under the rock.

---

255 Psalm 102:28

resolve

an invitation to lean on The Lover, not endlessly wander

"That we here highly resolve that these dead shall not have died in vain, that this nation, under God, shall have a new birth of freedom, and that government of the people, by the people, for the people, shall not perish from the earth."

-Abraham Lincoln

I can't decide what is worse. How ridiculous I feel or how much pain I am in? I started to feel the strain in my neck before bed last night. As a preventative, I took some Advil and a Panadol before going to sleep.

It didn't work.

Today the pain is worse. I can't look at either side of me without having to turn my whole body, hence I feel a tad silly as I have several social engagements today that require me to quickly turn and greet others. I make it through the morning and afternoon engagements. I even find some friends and have them pray for my neck. However, no change in my neck status.

It is not until the evening when I am at an Easter youth camp service that I begin to wonder if perhaps there is something more to my pain than just my body aging.

I want to leave, go home and rest, but feel the need to stay.

Many parents have responded to the invitation to come to their child's youth camp Easter service. I survey the parents; many are down-to-earth farming folk with impeccable reputations. Thus I am unsure what to think when I glance over at a gentleman that I have met only once or twice and immediately hear, "You stiff-necked people!"

I assume that I am in so much pain that I am now projecting onto this innocent bystander my state of being.

Yet, it won't leave. I keep hearing, "You stiff-necked people!"

Am I stiff-necked, Lord?

At the end of the evening, I return home, grab my concordance and look up 'You stiff-necked people!" The term implies stubbornness, a hard heartedness. It comes from the idea of unresponsive oxen or horses—beasts that are created and able to do a great work but refuse to bear the yoke of the plough.[256]

Do I resist the yoke of the plough?

"You stiff-necked people, with uncircumcised hearts and ears! You are just like your fathers: You always resist the Holy Spirit!"[257]

I read all kinds of commentaries and synthesize that a stiff-necked person is someone who is unyielding and that someone with an uncircumcised ear hears only what he or she wants to hear. I know I can be stubborn. Do I have selective hearing?

These words were spoken by Stephen, *a man full of God's grace and power, who did great wonders and miraculous signs among the people,*[258] to the Jewish religious leaders moments before they stoned him to death. Another incidence, I note, in which that religious bully seemed to win. I wonder what Stephen's words hit in them to make them so angry. I read the note in the commentary of my NIV bible, *"Though physically circumcised, they were acting like the uncircumcised pagan nations around them. They were not truly consecrated in their hearts."*[259]

Does anybody take kindly to being confronted with their own hypocrisy?

In my mind's eye, I survey the crowd and the Easter service the night before. I put the image together with what I have just read about being 'stiff-necked' and understand that although that man may have looked good and carried an untarnished reputation, God could see past his exterior. Like the Pharisees of Jesus day, the stiff-necked man looked good outwardly, but God wanted his heart. He had a form of religion, but his heart was stubborn, hard and or resistant to the Holy Spirit.

---

256 Biblestudytools.com, 'Stiff-necked,' accessed October 14, 2019, https://www. biblestudytools.com/dictionary/stiff-necked/
257 Acts 7:51
258 Acts 6:8
259 Commentary on Acts 7:51: Zondervan NIV Study Bible, Grand Rapids: Zondervan Publishing Company, 2008

But as I remember that crowded room, I also remember the acute pain I was feeling when I heard those words *stiff-necked* spoken. And I understand that unresolved emotional pain can cause stiffness and resistance to bear the yoke.

I look up like words for *yoke*: *harness, join, link, attach or connect*.[260]

And suddenly my questions take on a whole new meaning:

Where does unresolved emotional pain make me want to resist joining, linking, attaching or connecting with God? With others?

I understand that the gentleman with a stiff neck has a stubborn heart that is inclined to resist the Holy Spirit. But I also understand that God cares as much for the pain that disables the man from turning to see.

And I wonder, has this upside-down journey really been a means to begin to heal this kind of pain in me—pain that causes me to resist God's leading, His best?

Stephen's name for the Israelites was first coined by God himself several hundred years before. God had made a covenant with the people of Israel. Their marriage was binding and dependent on their faithfulness to each other. God kept his end of the promise. But the Israelites within a short time cheated on God. While Moses was away on the mountain receiving God's provisions and laws for his people, the Israelites made a golden calf to worship.

The Lord said to Moses, ***"I have seen these people and they are a stiff-necked people."*** [261]

God then tells Moses he wants to destroy them and start over via Moses. Moses intercedes on their behalf by seemingly reminding God of His own nature. And I am amused. Does God, the omnipotent, omniscient, omnipresent being need reminders? I can't help but wonder if God isn't playing devil's advocate here with Moses, the way I sometimes do with my kids to get them to realize the truth on their own? Is God really role-playing what Moses might say? And when Moses speaks, is **God not deeply affirming Moses' own understanding of God's heart?**

260 Dictionary.com, 'Yoke,' accessed October 12, 2019, https://www.dictionary.com/browse/yoked
261 Exodus 32:9

"God, why be angry with these slaves brought out of Egypt?" Moses reminds God that they are but slaves. They may be stiff-necked but remember that they have known pain. They are but slaves who have been subjected to a life of relentless work and abuse. It will not be easy for them to respond to God's great protection, provision and love; trust is built over time.

"God, do you want the Egyptians to think that you only delivered your people to destroy them?" Moses has seen God's true heart, 'gracious and compassionate, slow to anger and abounding in love.' God does not have evil intentions.

"And God, what about your promise to Abraham, Isaac and Jacob... to whom you swore by your own self?" Moses knows God to be a God who keeps His promises through the generations.

With that reminder, God agrees to continue to lead the people to the promised land. Upon reaching Kadesh Barnea, the outskirts of the promised land, the people rebel again. The scouts that had been sent out to spy on the land come back and give a negative report.

"We went into the land to which you sent us, and it does flow with milk and honey! ...But the people who live there are powerful, and the cities are fortified and very large. We even saw the descendant of Anak there... We seemed like grasshoppers in our own eyes, and we looked the same to them."[262]

The people encountered their own smallness but forgot to factor in God's bigness.

How big is my view of God?

After all the miraculous provision and protection God had shown them as a people, only two spies said the land could be taken. The other spies' talk spread fear throughout the people. Dread gripped the people. They were afraid that they were going to die in the desert or by the swords of the giants in the new land. The people then threatened Moses and talked about choosing a new leader who would lead them back to Egypt.

---

262 Numbers 13:27-28, 32b-33b

God held them accountable for their outright rejection of Him. Hence the people are told that they must wander in the desert until everyone of that generation dies. And I note that desert encounters can make us ask questions that lead to life or make us wander endlessly around and around until our death.

I do not want to wander aimlessly until my death.

I want to be like the beloved whom the friends say in Song of Solomon: *"Who is this coming up from the desert leaning on her lover?"*[263]

Forty years later the people come back to Kadesh Barnea. They come full circle to the place of their original rebellion and must face the very fear and enemy that they watched their parents encounter. Now it is their turn. What will they choose? Will they trust?

"Hear, O Israel. You are now about to cross the Jordan to go in and dispossess nations greater and stronger than you, with large cities that have walls up to the sky ... You know about them and have heard it said: "Who can stand up against the Anakites?" But be assured today that the Lord your God is the one who goes across ahead of you like a devouring fire. ...Understand, then, that it is not because of your righteousness that the Lord your God is giving you this good land to possess, for you are a stiff-necked people.[264]

My soul is pierced by these words.

I have been stiff-necked. I have been reluctant to connect with the people here, to do the things God has asked me to do. I have let old and deep fears dictate my steps; I would rather avoid than press in.

Forgive me, God.

I have recognized my own smallness here. But often I have forgotten God's vastness. I have entertained a lie that God might be impotent.

Wash me and I will be whiter than snow.[265]

Restore me, heal me.

---

263 Song of Solomon 8:5
264 Deuteronomy 9:1-3,6
265 Psalm 50:7b

Yes, I have come to a land full of the giants or bullies that I have found to be so destructive in my past. But God has promised this land to us. Why then should I shrink back? Why should I run from that *religious bully, the oppressive black spirit*, or even entertain the *shoulds*?

If I trust God, will He himself not go before me? I need not fear. Even should I perish, nothing is lost in eternity.

Of course, I am not good enough; it is not my righteousness that is going to win back the nation of New Zealand or any other for that matter.

Everything rides on God's terms: Jesus' faithfulness at the cross reveals God's ongoing faithfulness to mankind. Jesus is the face of God. Mercifully, it has never depended on our ability to keep the covenant. His love is not based on our human performance but on His unchangeable nature. He is simply looking for hearts turned towards him, hearts that are willing to dance with Him.

I feel no need to take license with this freedom, with this good news. I feel only humbled. My soul bows its knee before the greatness of God.

I hear the Lord proclaim his name before me.

And like Job, I am awed. I am silenced.

For this moment, all is still. There is a peace that says nothing can separate me from this kind of love.

Like Job, I want to say, I have heard of it, but I have now beheld it.

Like Esther, I want to say, If I perish, I perish, but let me obey and trust you to make the way.

I am reminded that I can obey and not trust. But I am learning to trust deeply and with that I now choose to obey.

Even if I should fail to do it perfectly right, like Elijah, God will uphold me. And it is He who will uphold and lead my children home.

"But the love of the Lord remains forever with those who fear him. His salvation extends to the children's children of those who are faithful to his covenant, of those who obey his commandments."[266]

---

266 Psalm 103:17-18

Once again the Lord's eyes are upon me, a gentle smile on his face... prodding my memory to words written at the beginning of this book:

"I hear the sound of a gentle warm breeze being overtaken by the roar of the engine, the thrill of my hands on the wheel next to Dad's, thinking that I was driving and the utter safety and security I felt resting in his arms."

Once again, the invitation to take such an adventure with the Lord is before me. Will I climb up into the vehicle He has chosen for me, put my hands on the wheel with His, and rest back into His arms?

Yes! At last I feel that I am ready. The Lord has patiently strolled me through my questions, doubts and fears to a place of deep trust; I have been invited into the sacred dance of a beautiful reciprocal relationship. From deep within flows a stream of gratitude not only for the "Lover of My Soul" but also for the beautiful man I called Father, who modelled this kind of love and trust to me.

the river

1. epilogue: a concluding part added to a literary work, as a novel.

2. river: any abundant stream or copious flow; outpouring.

"The Lord reached down from on high and took hold of me; he drew me out of the deep waters. He rescued me from my powerful enemy, from my foes, who were too strong for me. They confronted me in the day of my disaster, but the Lord was my support. He brought me out into a spacious place; he rescued me because he delighted in me."

-Psalm 18:16-19

I am humbled with a memory. When I began writing my questions down years ago, a woman I had just met came to me because she felt compelled to give me a verse from the book of Psalms along with some very lovely and encouraging words. She didn't know, I didn't even know that what I was writing would turn into this book, but she gave me these words as a commission:

"My heart bursts its banks, spilling beauty and goodness. I pour it out in a poem to the King, shaping the river into words."[267]

I wondered if she had heard right or gotten the wrong person. My questions didn't feel lovely. They didn't seep beauty but rather the decay of my heart. I didn't know that God would use them to *invite* me into knowing Him in a deeper and more beautiful way. Furthermore, the Psalmist's words were a mystery, "s*haping the river into words*"? I didn't understand.

I didn't understand what this verse meant until this last weekend, nearly five years later, when some friends took me away to Queenstown for a conference to hear one of my favourite speakers. Before the speaker got up, there was singing-time. The worship leader invited us to stand and 'step into' worship. Truthfully, the retort in my head was cynical,

---

267 Psalm 45:1 (MSG)

"What does that mean—to step into worship? Whatever!?" Still, I obeyed, stood to my feet and closed my eyes to hide my irritation.

In an instant, the eyes of my heart saw my feet step into a babbling brook; it was cool, refreshing. I thought to myself, "Oh, this is a delightful surprise." As if my delight granted the water permission, it came up higher; I was soon invigorated to my knees. Slowly the water began to rise and before I knew it, it was up to my neck. And I thought to myself, "Maybe, this isn't as fun as I thought!"

Should I panic? Should I get out?

Still the water captivated me and I felt powerless to leave. And then it did what I feared. It continued to rise until it had completely covered me. All I could think was, "I am in over my head." It felt as if I had been swallowed whole by the deep.

At first, I thrashed, trying to find my way back to the surface. To my dismay I didn't, couldn't, swim. I sunk to the bottom, certain that this would be the end of my life as I knew it. It was there that I found Jesus, right in front of me, looking at me. I felt ashamed that I couldn't swim these waters and I was afraid that I was going to die for lack of oxygen.

To my surprise, Jesus came face-to-face with me.

"My ears had heard of you but now my eyes have seen you."[268]

His lips sealed mine and His breath became my oxygen.

"Many waters cannot quench love; rivers cannot wash it away."[269]

He took me by the hand and taught me how to swim. It is weightless in the water; here I learned that I didn't need to perform. I was invited to play with Him.

This river that threatened to drown me has only proven that *Love* is stronger. *Love* endures.

I have been tested by deep waters and I know that they have forged in me a deeper, wider, longer and higher crevasse for the river of life to flow through me. I laugh when I read words recorded by Jesus:

---

268 Job 42:5
269 Song of Solomon 8:5

"When a woman gives birth, she has a hard time, there's no getting around it. But when the baby is born, there is joy in the birth. This new life in the world wipes out memory of the pain. The sadness you have right now is similar to that pain, but the coming joy is also similar. When I see you again, you'll be full of joy, and it will be a joy no one can rob from you. You'll no longer be so full of questions. "This is what I want you to do: Ask the Father for whatever is in keeping with the things I've revealed to you. Ask in my name, according to my will, and he'll most certainly give it to you. Your joy will be a river overflowing its banks![270]

I hear:

You are blessed when you come to understand your own poverty, then you can really see me.

You are blessed when you feel hungry, when the questions of life over power you, then I can feed you with the truth of who I am.

You are blessed when you feel sadness, when you weep, then you will be able to laugh and find joy.

You are blessed when others don't like you, because you are being freed from the self-imposed prison called "what will people think."

All at once I comprehend that my current soul journey through Antipodes is coming to an end. Simultaneously I gather that I am not leaving New Zealand, Antipodes has become my home. I have acclimated to living in this upside-down land; I have been called to live here.

Suddenly in my vision, quite steadily, I see that the waters begin to recede. It drains until I am seated on the floor like Edmond and Lucy in The Voyage of the Dawn Treader.[271] The adventure is over and I note that my clothes aren't wet, not even damp.

I see the Lord before me. He looks deeply into my eyes, puts his hand on my shoulder and says, "You're fine!"

Dazed, I adjust my gaze to His eyes and repeat, "I'm fine."

---

270 John 16:21-24 (MSG)
271 Henley, Georgie and Keynes, Skandar. *Narnia: Voyage of the Dawn Trader.* DVD. Directed by Michael Apted. Los Angeles, 20th Century Fox Studios, 2010

As I look at the Lord's eyes, they start to dance mischievously, daringly, as if there is another adventure to be had. He glances back over his shoulder; in the distance I see a path of hot coals for us to walk.

"Really, God?"

I flashback to the day after my son was born. My husband was holding him, beaming with great joy, when he looked up and said, "When can we have another one?" Pleased that my husband was happy with the outcome but somewhat wanting to remind him of the pain I had been through just twenty-four hours before, I said with a hint of sarcasm in my voice, "Could I get over yesterday first?"

The feeling is similar when I look at the Lord, "Okay, I see the great worth of where we have walked, but could I get over the last five years please before we plunge into the next adventure?"

I think of this landscape I have been traversing called Antipodes and realise that it has taught me how to navigate deep waters. It is the understanding of these deep waters, of this river that I have been slowly and surely *shaping into words.*

Slowly but surely, I have been transformed by this process, by this journey across Antipodes.

I have been humbled by the depths of my own poverty, my own weaknesses. Religion left me feeling condemned, kept telling me to pull it together. But I am discovering a loving God whose arms are big and strong enough to save me from myself.

I have felt the gnawing hunger for answers and have been satisfied by a God who is willing to dialogue. He is not easily angered nor daunted by my questions.

In my mess, in my weeping, I have been learning to release what I can't fix, explain, understand or control. Instead I am learning to embrace life in all its varied moments.

And I have faced deep fears, oppressive giants in my own soul that made me reluctant to embrace Truth.

It dawns on me that through this adventure, God has become my Captain. Like my father, I trust him to have my back, offer sound leadership advice, lead the way home and make a way to see me, his girl.

With this ultimate reality, I can feel curiosity arising in me. I wonder what that trail of fire in the distance might represent? What kingdom truths might I learn there? And with a giggle, I mutter under my breath, "Well…at least it will be warmer! Maybe we won't need too long a break in between; I might get bored."

And then I hear a voice laugh, a voice I have come to love and trust…

"Shall we?"

And once again I take His hand, wondering what kind of steps I might learn on the fire trail. I know now, in the depths of my soul, that God is more than enough and that together we will navigate whatever terrain lies before us.

Acknowledgments

First, I want to thank the beautiful people of Gore, New Zealand, for the kindness and generosity they showed me while trying to figure out this new land. It is impossible to convey how each of you touched my heart in a way that I am forever changed. In particular, I thank my dearest friends from there; my 'Walking Encyclopedia', my 'Critical Balance', my 'Grounding,' my surrogate 'Sister' and 'Brother' for your love and support not only while in Gore but also in the making of this book.

In addition, I could not have made it through this leg of the journey without the 'Sequoia Roots' friendships from back home. I am blessed by the depth of our friendship that surpasses time and space; the roots forged in eternity.

Thank you to my family of origin who have taken parallel journeys across the world. Mom, you have endured so many losses and faced such pain —truly you are the bravest woman I know. Thank you for your unconditional love, for modeling such a deep love for Jesus, and for being the first to say that these pages were meant to be shared with others. Rachel, a remnant, you stayed fixed as everything in your world left or fell apart. I marvel at the pluck you have shown in gathering, holding together, and forging new ways forward. Thank you for always making a way for us to see each other again. Michael, I have such a deep respect for how different our journeys have been and continue to learn from your insight and desire for authenticity. Thank you for pushing me beyond societal norms. A great big thank you to my husband and children who remained flexible and supportive as I saw this project through editing and publishing. I am so blessed by your faithful love. Bruce, thanks for loving me even in the messy times and for never allowing life to be boring! Thank you to my friends that read earlier manuscripts and gave me valuable feedback. Particularly, I am most grateful to Pam Williamson, Jessie Minassian, Stella Snaddon, Craig Roberts, Nina Peck,Brendon Harrex, Betty Fry and Peri Zahnd for the hours you spent in helping to edit and encourage this project forward. Finally, a great big thank you to Bernard Harris and Wild Goose Publishing. It has been a pleasure to work with you. I appreciate your passion, vision and integrity to capture the voices of 'warrior poets and rebel writers' into print. What an absolute privilege to chase the Wild Goose together.